THE G.L.O.W PRINCIPLE

A Step-by-Step Blueprint to Empower Black Women in Leadership

ERIKA RAE BAILEY

Copyright and Disclosures

Mango Broom Ltd

Email: sparkle@mangobroom.com

ISBN 978-1-913937-04-1 (eBook)

ISBN 978-1-913937-05-8 (print book)

First Edition

Legal and Disclaimer. Please note the information contained within this book is for educational and entertainment purposes only.

Furthermore, the information contained in this book and its contents is not designed to replace or take the place of any form of medical, psychological, or professional advice; and it is not meant to replace the need for independent medical, financial, legal, or other professional advice or services as may be required. The content and information in this book have been provided for educational and entertainment purposes only.

The content and information contained in this book have been compiled from sources deemed reliable, and it is accurate to the best of the Publisher's and Author's knowledge, information, and belief. However, the Publisher or Author cannot guarantee its accuracy and validity and cannot be held liable for any errors and/or omissions. Further, changes are periodically made to this book as and when needed. Where appropriate and/or necessary, you must consult a professional (including but not limited to your doctor, attorney, financial advisor, or such other professional advisor) before using any of the suggested remedies, techniques, or information in this book.

Upon using the contents and information contained in this book, you agree to hold harmless the Publisher and Author from and against any damages, costs, and expenses, including any legal fees potentially resulting from the application of any information provided in this book. This disclaimer applies to any loss, damages, or injury caused by the use and application, whether directly or indirectly, of any advice or information presented, whether for breach of contract, tort, negligence, personal injury, criminal intent, or under any other cause of action.

You agree to accept all risks of using the information presented inside this book.

You agree by continuing to read this book that, where appropriate and/or necessary, you shall consult a professional (including but not limited to your doctor, attorney, financial advisor, or other such professional advisors) before using any of the suggested remedies, techniques, or information in this book. Reading the information in this book does not create a physician-patient relationship.

While many experiences related in this book are true, names and identifying details have been changed to protect the privacy of individuals.

Get FREE Books Before They Are Released!

Join the Insider's Club and we will email you **FREE** copies of new books before we publish them.

You may ask, why would we give away our books for **FREE**?

Well, our ***VIP Insider Club Members*** help us greatly with fine-tuning a book before it goes on general release.

We value any feedback and input provided, whenever it is needed. We have some of the best editors in the business, but now and then, our eagle-eyed Insider Club Members will spot something that could do with a little tweaking…thanks in advance!

We publish non-fiction and fiction books, from business, self-help and health books to children's stories and romance novels.

Click (or tap) below to JOIN the exclusive **VIP Insider Club Members** and start receiving FREE Books before they are published.

Click here:
https://www.mangobroom.com/insiders-club/

CONTENTS

INTRODUCTION

I DECIDED TO START glowing a few years ago. You see, everyone around me thinks I am this strong, awesome woman who is capable of doing everything. Indeed, I am. But there has been a lot holding me back.

How can I embrace who I am as a black woman without ruffling some feathers?

Viewing black in its purest form paints a clear picture of what it represents—power, elegance, strength and mystery. This is who we are as black women.

We are oozing with the power of melanin that makes our dark chocolate scream with sheer delight about the power we represent. We are resilient, bold, a catalyst for change and the epitome of a Nubian queen clothed in strength and dignity.

> "I'm convinced that we black women possess a special indestructible strength that allows us to not only get down, but to get up, to get through and to get over."
> ~Janet Jackson

Shout it from the rooftops! Sing it on the hills! Black don't crack, girl! Even when we are down and out, we have an indestructible strength that helps us rise up even stronger than before, a strength that helps us ***glow***.

That is where the problem starts to worm its way in. I am unapologetically me; proud to be a bold, authentic woman who changes lives and builds a strong family.

However, my coworkers (and other naysayers) try to dim my light. My girl, Maura Cheeks, understands what I am talking about. Granted, I have never met this woman, but I identify with what she wrote in her Harvard Business Review article entitled *How Black Women Describe Navigating Race and Gender in the Workplace.*

She interviewed ten black women in the corporate world. These women highlighted four grave challenges they faced:

- Reducing personalities (dimming their light) so that they fit in.
- Difficulty of finding someone in the workplace who is in your corner.

- Coworkers being unable to relate to issues unique to a black woman.
- Being inauthentic while at work but authentic around friends.

WTH!

Why should I become inauthentic to fit in with the status quo? Why should I put out my flame because it makes others uncomfortable?

My decision to G.L.O.W was my answer to these questions. About two years ago, I decided to make a deliberate effort to step into my greatness as a resilient black woman and prepare myself for bigger and better things.

I wrote this book to help you embrace this G.L.O.W principle and leverage it for a brighter future. Your black strength will only shine if you understand how to G.L.O.W it up! Are you ready to:

G: ***Game*** plan and vision.
L: ***Leap*** into your passion.
O: ***Own*** your power.
W: ***Walk*** into your destiny?

Put your game face on, grab yourself a nice cup of black coffee and prepare for this book to give you that special glow. You will not only learn how to find your inner strength, but you will also be guided through thought-provoking questions that help you dive deep into paving a path of greatness.

Strength also does not negate weakness. Like any

woman on this planet, you are probably grappling with internal struggles that only you know about. You are probably afraid to show any signs of weakness for fear that they will lead to your demise.

It is okay to need a mental break, want to be pampered, understand your limitations and cry those ugly tears. This book will help you understand how to bounce back from these down moments quickly as you seek to balance your career (or business) with the responsibilities of taking care of your family and, above all, taking care of you.

Your power as a black woman should not be stifled. There is so much value that you can gain from glowing it up, and you should not be forced to dim your light.

This is not a joy ride that gives you a momentary thrill and leaves you with prolonged sadness. Instead, it is a ticket for the journey of your life that will take you onto paths undiscovered and opportunities that you never thought possible. It is your life; how will you make it count? What will your story be?

This book is a resource that will only work well if you:

1. Read each chapter.
2. Complete the reflection questions found at the end of each chapter.
3. Put what you have written into action.
4. Keep track of your progress.

Each section attempts to answer some challenging life questions.

Part One: The Game Plan

1. What thoughts are holding you back?
2. How can you create a tribe of mentors?
3. How can you create better circumstances?
4. What does my life's vision look like?

Part Two: The Leap

1. How can you transform your passion into profit?
2. What is the value of your personal brand?
3. How can you look beyond black stereotypes and glow in your own light?

Part Three: Own Your Power

1. How can you become a successful entrepreneur?
2. How can you leverage your online presence to increase your sphere of influence?
3. What are the four powerful habits you need to develop to help you to grow stronger, faster?

Part Four: Walk Into Your Destiny

1. Who should be the one standing by your side?
2. How can you be consistent?
3. How can you maintain your focus in the midst of distraction?

The answers to these questions are right here in this book. Those who will benefit the most from this book are black women who are:

- Ready for change.
- Confident in who they are and who they can become.
- Ready to embrace their true calling.
- Proud of their Nubian heritage.
- Open to embracing the power of sisterhood.
- Ready to step into their vision, even if the first steps are tiny.

Are you this woman?

Join me on this wonderful ride of self-discovery, empowerment, and preparation for a brighter future. I cannot wait to share my personal experiences with you, and I hope that they will inspire you to glow instead of dimming your light.

Let's get started!

PART 1

The Game Plan

"There have been so many people who have said to me, 'You can't do that,' but I've had an innate belief that they were wrong. Be unwavering and relentless in your approach."
~Halle Berry

CHAPTER 1

Silence the Noise

> "You become what you believe. You are where you are today in your life based on everything you have believed."
>
> ~Oprah Winfrey

My mother taught me two important lessons—stand up for yourself and get a good education. She was never one to encourage a fist fight, but she knew how to stand up for me with her voice and the words that she penned in strong letters of concern to the powers that be who did me wrong. I also watched her work extremely hard to get her PhD at the age of 54, a degree she now uses to make a difference in our community.

Her example and support have helped me become the woman I am today; a woman who people respect because of her intellect and quiet way of inspiring change. People think I am strong, creative and capable of doing anything I set my mind to.

Little do they know that I have fought with many mental demons. The woman they see today is the result of an ongoing mental battle that I never thought I would win. However, it is a battle I knew I had to win if I wanted to glow in a way that matters.

My Mental Battle

I am an only child who was raised by her single mother and her grandmother (mother's mother). Without even realizing it, living without my father as a constant presence in my life impacted how I behaved and perceived myself. Add the fact that my grandmother once told me that my father never wanted me, and my feelings of self-worth went down the drain.

As a teenager, I buried my head in my schoolwork because I knew that I had to depend on my intellect to take me somewhere. I got As and Bs and even placed top in my class at various points in high school, but I still always felt very average, like nothing I did would ever be good enough no matter how hard I tried.

Thankfully, my mother raised me with strong values which prevented me from straying away in search of love and acceptance. I found a great group of friends who are like sisters to me and have been my friends for the past 18 years. They helped me to better appreciate who I am and the value I bring to this world.

However, a mental battle kept waging in my mind as I grew into a young adult. My "I am just average" mentality seemed to have been reinforced when my application for medical school was rejected. You see, my grades were just okay—nothing spectacular, like some of my peers.

I felt defeated because the intellect that I was depending on to take me somewhere had suddenly failed. My mind began to take a further dive into a really dark place, and I became more comfortable hiding within my shell.

As if things could not get any worse, I woke up one day in my room at the university I was attending and saw a deep sink in one side of my face! The doctor at the university's health center told me that there was nothing that could be done and rudely said, "At least you won't be entering any beauty pageants."

Another blow to my already damaged self-esteem.

Years later, I would find out that I have a rare case of facial atrophy. Simply put, fat spontaneously disappeared from one section of my face. There is no cure and anything that a plastic surgeon does will only be temporary. So, I live daily with a huge sink in one side of my face.

I was facing all of these mental battles while being an active leader on campus and pursuing a BSc in Mathematics with Education. I would wake up each day, do what I had to do, laugh a bit, and have some fun while being constantly hammered by a barrage of negative thoughts.

- Why am I not good enough?
- Guys who find me attractive are lying.

- I just have to settle with whatever life throws at me.
- I will never achieve the success I have dreamt about since I was a little girl.
- Why was I even born?

These thoughts were crippling. Sure, I was inspired to wake up each day and do something with my life because my drive to motivate and inspire others was (and still is) powerful. Yet, these thoughts always found a way to creep into my subconscious and fill me with fear so crushing that I let opportunities slip by.

Not anymore!

I decided to change my thinking about two years ago.

> "Change your thinking, change your life! Your thoughts create your reality. Practice positive thinking. Act the way you want to be, and soon you will be the way you act."
> ~ Les Brown

My Process of Mental Change

I think I was about 15 years old when I read Myles Munroe's book "Understanding Your Potential" and it struck a chord in me. Although I was still facing my mental battles, I began to view my life differently the moment I finished reading that book.

There is a specific quote in the book that has stuck with me till this day. It says,

> "The graveyard is the richest place on earth because there you will see the books that were not published, ideas that were not harnessed, songs that were not sung, and drama pieces that were never acted. Don't contribute to the wealth of the graveyard."
> ~Myles Munroe

Have you ever thought about the graveyard that way?

The magnitude of Monroe's statement resonated with me. I do not want to contribute to the wealth of the graveyard!

Two years ago, I began to reminisce on my life. I looked back at all I had accomplished and all that I have left to do. It slowly dawned on me that I needed to do some spring cleaning on my mind before I ended up contributing to the richest place on earth.

And, girl, that was a life-changing moment for me! I

needed to get rid of some cobwebs hiding in the crevices of my mind. Here's what I did.

1. I spoke with my dad.

This was probably one of the most difficult things I had to do. I spent about three months last year trying to meet with my dad in person to talk through some of the thoughts that had been bothering me for most of my life. We were always missing each other but we finally met in October.

I don't think I really poured my heart out but I did ask some questions for which I needed answers. My dad is cool and he has always provided for me the best way he could financially despite not being around to raise me. So, he listened to me, shared his thoughts and gave some words of encouragement.

I felt released.

Released from over ten years of emotional baggage and daddy issues.

Released from feelings of being unworthy and unwanted.

Released from thoughts of just calling it quits on this thing called life.

This release empowered me. It helped me feel like a void in my heart had been filled. My mind's cobwebs were vanishing.

2. I reframed my thinking.

The process of reframing my thinking began a little more than two years ago, if my memory serves me correctly. Girl, I am aging like fine wine so I cannot keep track of these dates sometimes!

Anyways, I developed this nifty way of changing my negative thoughts into positive thoughts because I honestly do not believe that we ever really completely get rid of the occasional negative thought. Here is how I flipped the script:

1. Each time I felt a negative thought coming into my head I would tell myself (in my head, of course) to, "Hold up!"
2. Those two words force me to pause and really consider what I am thinking.
3. I then say this with a bit of attitude, "Put that lie in the trash and take that smile out the bag!"
4. I then reword the negative statement so that it has a positive, rather than a negative, tone.

I know that it sounds like a lot of steps, but I literally do this within about 10 seconds.

Let me demonstrate with an example. Let us say that this thought comes into my head: "I'm not good enough." This is how my self-talk works.

1. Hold up! You think you are not good enough?!
2. Put that lie in the trash and take that smile out the bag!
3. You are good enough and can become the best

> if you continue to hone your skills and put in the work. You have got this!

See what I did there?

Following this trend has helped me become a more positive person. In fact, it has empowered me to accept who I am so that I can be a light for others. Trust me, it is a blessing.

3. I talked to those in my inner circle.

Too often, I was trying to fight the demons in my head alone. There are nights when I would cry myself to sleep and just lay in the darkness from as early as 7:00 pm because the thoughts were overwhelming.

However, I have learnt over the past two years that my futile attempts to fight this battle alone were getting me nowhere. There are about three people in my inner circle who I trust with my life. I have been sharing my thoughts and fears with these people and they have truly been blessings in helping me clean out the cobwebs in my mind.

> "Friendship makes prosperity more brilliant, and lightens adversity by dividing and sharing it."
> ~Cicero

What does this mean for you?

You have your own mental cobwebs. Getting rid of those cobwebs is the only way for you to truly begin the glowing process with a solid game plan. It will not be easy, and you should accept the fact that it is an ongoing process.

But you are a powerful black woman whose strength is limitless. ***You've got this!*** I have created the R-E-A-C-H strategy to help you get through this because I want you to reach for those cobwebs and ***tear them down***.

The R-E-A-C-H Strategy

R - Release your baggage.

The process of silencing the noise in your head begins with a process of releasing the weight that is on your heart. This stage is not about confronting those who you need answers from. Instead, it is about being honest with yourself about the baggage you carry.

Some women are easily able to identify this baggage. However, you may be one of those women who has been hiding it for so long that you do not even know exactly what it is anymore. You have been putting on a façade for too long.

But you have still got to dig deep and find the root cause of your hurt, the weight that is holding you down. Once you have found it, you need to release those emotions and put them behind you. Cry and scream in the bathroom if you have to but just ***let those emotions out***.

It is okay for you to give yourself permission to just feel and release.

E - Engage in dialogue.

This step may not be applicable to everyone because the people who have wronged you may either be long gone or unwilling to engage in dialogue. However, there are some of us who can get answers from people we feel have hurt us most.

Those answers can be liberating. Engaging my father in dialogue was a cathartic experience for me. Sometimes, this dialogue is exactly what you need to clear out some of those mental cobwebs.

A - Appreciate who you are (and who you can become).

Self-love is crucial. You must appreciate who you are (both good and bad). This acceptance challenges you to reject the negative thoughts that will continue to flood your head. It also helps you understand that you do not need to be perfect (no one is) and you can be unapologetically you.

However, this does not mean that you should become comfortable with your negative traits. It is not okay to say, "That's just who I am." It is important to be open to the constructive criticism people will share with you (or even the negative things that you have identified about yourself) and use that to become an even better you. Life is about learning and growing.

"It was when I realized I needed to stop trying to be somebody else and be myself that I actually started to own, accept and love what I had."
~Tracee Ellis Ross

C - Control your thoughts.

Les Brown aptly said that when you change your thinking, you change your life. It is important for you to realize that you control your thoughts; your thoughts do not control you. I find that this process of controlling your thoughts is very personal so you should take some time finding a strategy that works for you. You are welcome to use the strategy that I developed, if you'd like!

H - Hold on to your inner circle.

It is difficult to fight this battle alone. You should trust that your inner circle is your best bet at supporting your journey towards silencing the noise in your head. Although they have their own challenges, they are still willing to listen and provide the best support they can give. That is what friends are for!

A strong game plan is built from a strong mind.

You are the product of your thoughts. There may be cobwebs in your mind that need to be cleaned out before you can shine your brightest light. The thought of dying without fulfilling my purpose scares me because I really do not want to contribute to the wealth of the graveyard. Do you feel the same?

I want you to R-E-A-C-H for those cobwebs and remove them from your mind. Trust me, it is an empowering process that helps you better understand who you are, how you think and how you can create a positive mind that strengthens your game plan.

REFLECTION QUESTIONS

1. What negative thoughts constantly pop up in your mind?
2. How has applying the R-E-A-C-H strategy helped you deal with those thoughts?
3. What feedback have you gotten from the people in your inner circle?

CHAPTER 2

A New Vision

> "My mission in life is not merely to survive, but to thrive; and to do so with some passion, some compassion, some humor, and some style."
>
> ~Maya Angelou

It was a cold November morning in Bronx, New York. I rubbed my eyes gently as they adjusted to the dim winter morning light. My matchbox apartment had a view of the streets below and I could already sense that those streets were filled with people rushing from one place to the next. Horns were blaring, people were cursing, and it was only 7:00 am.

It had been a year since I had been offered a contract to work with a growing online education company. As a young, black woman raised in Florida, this was a new and exciting experience for me. The hustle and bustle, exciting party scene and never-ending list of things to do thrilled me.

I also enjoyed using what I learned from my BSc in Mathematics with Education degree to create engaging and impactful lessons for the company's 5,000 online students. It finally felt like I was able to do something useful with the degree I never really wanted in the first place.

But something was missing. As I opened the tiny kitchen window in my apartment, it hit me. I had been basing my life and my future on a lie.

You see, I was telling myself that this was all my life was chalked up to be. I would keep working in this "stable" job even if it did not truly make me feel complete because it offered benefits. I wanted to show that my degree was not a waste of time.

I was also working in an environment that was not the best for a young, black woman, unashamed of her appearance and strength. There were only two black girls in the office—me and another lady who worked in HR. I had probably only seen her once since I had been at the company.

Now, don't get me wrong. I had established myself as a valuable member of the team. After all, I had helped them develop a proprietary strategy for helping slow learners grasp fundamental math concepts. However, it was not without much fight back from my superiors. It sometimes felt like they wanted me to fail so they could prove that the little black girl from Florida was not worth their time. They wanted to keep me well placed in the "inferior basket".

They seemed nice enough on the surface. The work environment was pretty laid back and it was customary for us to go out for drinks together at least once a month at a bar two blocks down.

I just could not shake the feeling that they did not look beyond my skin color to appreciate who I was as a strong, independent woman. Sometimes I wondered if I was only there to have the box ticked for the company's ethnicity quota.

As I stared through my tiny kitchen window at the walls of the apartment building across the street, I remembered a recent conversation I had with my supervisor. We had an amicable relationship and she had mentored me when I was still a newbie. But what she said during this conversation made me view her differently.

She said, "I never thought that a young, black girl like you would make it this far. You are making waves in the company and people are starting to take notice. It looks like my mentorship paid off."

A young, black girl like me?

What did that have to do with anything? Hadn't I proven that I was smart, innovative and able to take the initiative needed to effect change? What was so wrong with me that I could not be seen as the woman I am instead of being labeled as the black girl from Florida?

On this cold November morning, I decided that it was time for me to change my narrative. No longer would

I be trapped by my circumstances and force myself to hide in a shell.

No longer will I just fit in when I can lead. No longer will I roll with the status quo when I can crush it. I am going to put my head above the parapet.

It was time for a new vision.

> "Instead of letting your hardships and failures discourage or exhaust you, let them inspire you."
> ~Michelle Obama

What is vision?

Sanjiva Weerawarana, in an article entitled *What is Vision and Why is It Important to Have Personal Vision*, defined vision as "the ability to close your eyes and imagine a future that does not yet exist. It is the ability to see beyond the mess that may be in front of you, to abstract away from it, to clean it up and see a (hopefully better) future that does not yet exist."

Think back to when you were a child. Your big imagination would probably take you on adventures in distant lands that you could only see in your head. The fantasies you created seemed so real that it was difficult for you to listen to the adults who told you otherwise.

Your vision will fall somewhere between reality and

fantasy. Although it is developed through careful planning and preparation, your vision will paint a picture of something that ***seems*** impossible within the constraints of your present circumstances.

It is something that you need to believe is possible, deep within your heart and soul. Granted, you are not going to blindly step into this idyllic world that you have created in the same way you would if you were still a child. I will explain the practical approach I took to revise my vision and guide you through the steps you can take to do the same.

My Visioning Process

I was eager for the weekend to come so that I could devote some time to charting a new course for my life. All I had was a blank sheet of cartridge paper and random thoughts bursting through my mind.

My brainstorming produced the diagram below.

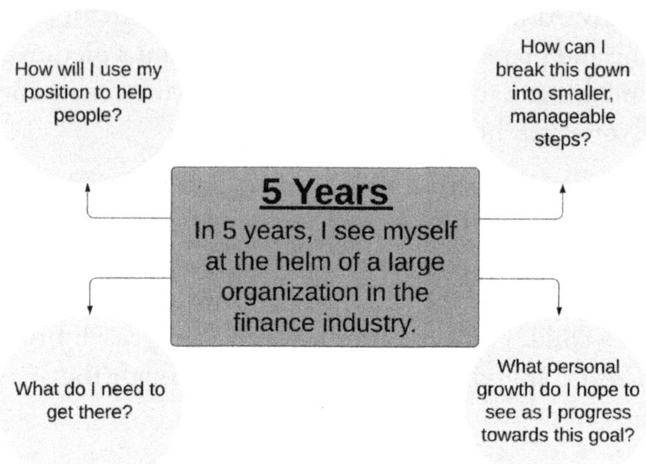

I made a deliberate attempt to chart a 5-year vision for my life. It was a vision sparked by my interest in investments and how I could help people become better managers of their personal finances.

How will I use my future position to help people?

I truly believe that not contributing to the wealth of the graveyard is more than just me making the best use of my skills. Instead, it is about using my skills in the best way possible to add value to the lives of other people.

While creating this brainstorming chart, I envisioned myself in my power executive suit, strutting my stuff down the hallways of a financial firm that would appreciate me for who I am and what I bring to the table.

I also envisioned myself creating a financial literacy program for kids; that would be my way of giving back to the world. That is how I would use my position (and influence) to help people.

What do I need to get there?

I knew that becoming a top-level finance executive would not be a simple feat. I had also heard horror stories about the cutthroat nature of the finance industry. Yet, I still believed that was where I needed to be.

So, I began thinking about what I would need to get to that top-level position. I would need:

- A Master's degree or a professional certification such as the CFA.
- Experience in the industry.
- A network of people in the profession.

What personal growth do I hope to see as I progress towards this goal?

Some of my character traits needed to change if I wanted to step up in the world of finance. I knew that I needed to stop taking on a confident persona and start working on building genuine confidence. Additionally, it would be important for me to get comfortable with networking and meeting new people.

How can I break this down into smaller, manageable steps?

It becomes more difficult to manifest a vision when it is viewed as one big project. As the saying goes, the best way to eat an elephant is by taking bitesize chunks. These bitesize chunks would become my goals.

My vision needed to be broken down into smaller, manageable steps (goals) so that I could track my progress and make adjustments where necessary.

Here is how I broke things down.

Year 1: Get an entry-level job at a finance firm.

- Save at least $10,000 so that I can leave my current job within six to eight months.
- Find out where finance professionals hang out in New York, attend some of their events and meet new people.
- Connect with finance professionals in the area on LinkedIn and express interest in applying for a job in the field.

Year 2: Enroll in a professional certification or Master's program.

- Determine the field of finance I am most interested in within six months of my first finance job.
- Thoroughly research the educational requirements to enter that finance niche.
- Apply to relevant programs.

- Begin classes in the winter semester.
- Find a mentor.

Year 3: Get a promotion.

- Move from an entry-level to a mid-level position.
- Participate in outreach programs so that I can holistically develop my skills and make a difference in my community.
- Continue professional qualifications (I may be in a program that either lasts for two or three years).

Year 4: Create a financial literacy for kids program.

- Use the knowledge and experience gained over the past three years to develop a financial literacy for kids program for kids in New York.
- Continue to participate in community projects.
- Continue professional qualifications.

Year 5: Become a top-level financial professional.

- Complete professional qualifications and apply for a top-level position.
- Make the financial literacy program national.

I won't bore you with how I broke these smaller steps down even further to a month-by-month task list.

However, there is a part of my visioning process that I cannot omit—my vision board. If I am completely honest, I have been skeptical of vision boards ever since I first heard about them about five or six years ago.

I think my perspective changed when someone I know mentioned creating a vision board each year to the point where she now had a series of vision boards on her wall. She mentioned feeling more motivated to accomplish her goals so that her annual vision could be realized. Sure, some things would carry over from one year to the next, but maintaining this momentum helped her accomplish far more than she would have without the vision boards.

So, I knew that I had to approach creating a new vision for my life differently. I needed to let go of my skepticism and give this vision board thing a shot.

The beauty of a vision board is that it helps you clearly visualize what you want to achieve. The focus is on images rather than words which ultimately leads to better retention of what you are trying to achieve.

Research conducted by scientists at the Massachusetts Institute of Technology (MIT) proved that the human brain can process images in as little as 13 milliseconds. It is believed that it takes twice as long to process text.

Therefore, writing my vision and goals was insufficient. I went to an art supplies store a few blocks from my apartment and purchased an 8 by 8 cotton canvas, some decorative pieces (glitter, stickers, letters and other knickknacks), glue, scissors and some decorative markers. On my way back home, I bought some newspapers and magazines at a kiosk.

I spent about three hours that evening putting the vision board for my five-year vision together. It had pictures that represented everything I needed to accomplish to reach my ultimate goal. I then hung it on the wall directly in front of my bed so that it would be the first thing I saw when I woke up each morning.

This is essentially how I spent that chilly November weekend creating a new vision for my life.

How can you create a new vision?

You do not want to spend your life trying to survive from one day to the next. Regardless of your current circumstances, you are meant to thrive and leave a lasting imprint on this world. It is time to step away from that situation that has been putting out your fire for far too long.

It is time to change your narrative. Have you subjected yourself to the limitations life has placed on you? No more, girl, no more.

I do not know the nature of your unique situation. You could be trapped in an abusive relationship, stuck in a job, struggling to make ends meet despite having three jobs, trying your best to balance raising a child on your own...whatever it is, it is time for you to say, "Enough!"

You have the power to flip the script. You have the power to create a new vision for your life.

It all starts with writing things down. Do not keep it in your head. ***Write it down.***

These are the questions you should answer.

1. What is your five-year vision for the five dimensions of your life?

   I only focused on one dimension in my example. However, we are multi-faceted beings who are not bound to our careers. Use a separate sheet of paper for each of these five dimensions:

   - Spirituality (if you are spiritual).
   - Family.
   - Health.
   - Career.
   - Finances.

2. Ask yourself five questions as you think carefully about these five dimensions:

   a. How can I help people?
   b. What do I need to get there?
   c. What personal growth do I hope to see as I progress towards this goal?
   d. Who will I need to become in order to achieve my goals?
   e. How can I break this down into smaller, more manageable steps?

3. Create your vision board.

Don't live in the clouds.

It is great to have a vision that helps us feel like we can accomplish anything. We are often told that we should dream big and that anything is possible as long as we believe.

All of that is true, but it is also important to be practical. Your vision guides your life, but it is also driven by the small, actionable steps that you take each day. Therefore, it is important for you to create manageable goals that are SMARTER.

You have probably already heard about SMARTER goals multiple times. But I am still giving you a refresher because you need to pay attention to it so that you do not create an unattainable vision for your life.

S - Specific.

M - Measurable.

A - Attainable.

R - Relevant.

T - Time-bound.

E - Evaluated.

R - Reviewed.

Here is how I could have made my five-year vision SMARTER.

In five years, I will be in the top 10 percent of leaders in the financial industry. I will be the founder and CEO of Melona Financial Group, a financial company that will be included in the Inc 100 Fastest-Growing Companies by year four. Through my creativity and influence, I will teach at least one million children across America with my financial literacy program. I will evaluate my progress towards this goal quarterly, and make adjustments where necessary.

How can you make your five-year vision and your smaller goals SMARTER?

Will it be smooth sailing?

No. There will be times when you are going to feel like giving up, when you want to tear your hair out, when you wonder why you ever decided to go down this road in the first place...but that is the beauty of the journey.

There will also be times when you will fail, miserably. How you deal with that failure is ultimately what matters. Will you give up and throw your vision through the window or will you become stronger because of it?

> "Your ability to adapt to failure, and navigate your way out of it, absolutely 100 percent makes you who you are."
> ~Viola Davis

We will discuss navigating failure later in this book. However, it is important to mention it here because the journey towards achieving your vision will be riddled with failure. Prepare for it.

The right vision creates a solid game plan.

Blavity is a tech company created by black female powerhouse, Morgan Debaun. The company began in 2014 as an online community for black creativity and news. She wanted it to be a platform for black people who are treated like outsiders and are looked down upon; she wanted the world to see that ***we all matter***.

With this singular focus, the Blavity team worked assiduously towards creating a community of economic and creative support for black millennials across the African diaspora. Their support has allowed black millennials to pursue the work they love and become catalysts for change in their communities. Since then, the company has raised over $10 million from angel investors.

However, Debaun and her team recently decided to reframe their strategy. The company has expanded to become Blavity Inc which now focuses on creating a ***world*** where ***all*** black people are ***happy***.

Her story demonstrates how creating a vision that adds value to society leads to a solid game plan. It also demonstrates that this vision will need some revision as you evolve and gain new experiences.

Be like Debaun and create an exciting vision that will not only empower you, but also one that will empower others; one that will help you to make your own little dent in the universe.

REFLECTION QUESTIONS

1. What are the pros and cons of your current situation?
2. What small, manageable changes can you make now to get rid of the negative aspects of your current environment?
3. How can your five-year vision help you make a lasting impact on the world?
4. When you manifest your vision, how will it impact your life?

CHAPTER 3

Build a Network of Sisters

> "The success of every woman should be the inspiration to another. We should raise each other up."
>
> -Serena Williams

ANGER QUICKLY TRANSFORMED into rage as America's black community responded to the wrongful death of George Floyd in May 2020. Just when we think that people are getting the message that black lives ***do*** matter, there comes another report which demonstrates the height of racism.

Ahmaud Arbery, Michael Brown, Freddie Gray, Philando Castile, Alton Sterling… a never-ending list of the fatalities from nonsensical racial acts.

But these names represent a trend; one that is particularly frightening to me as a black woman trying to navigate this complex world. Most of these acts of racism are directed towards ***black men***.

I am not a mother, but I act like a second mother to the

little black girls and boys of my friends and relatives. How can I teach these beautiful black children to live without fear and believe that their dreams are possible in this racially divided world?

How can I as a ***black woman*** demonstrate that it is not a matter of black and white, but it's a matter of plain disregard for the fact that all human beings have red blood running through their veins?

It starts by building a network of sisters.

Sisters who support each other in raising strong black ladies and gentlemen who, despite the odds stacked against them, still make a powerful impact on this world.

Sisters who support each other's visions.

Sisters who demonstrate that strength comes from having a unified voice.

Sisters who believe that it is not okay to be silent about the issues we face because of the color of our skin.

As black women, we need to stand up together as sisters and embody the world in which we want to live. A world where our success is not rare and where we are seen as equals to people of other races.

The Strength of a Black Female Mentor

In 2018, I took on a new role as a business analyst at a small financial firm in lower Manhattan. There was a mature black woman who I looked forward to seeing each day. She ran the financial services division and proudly sported her thick, black afro each day she came to work.

Her flawless skin seemed to almost glow and she commanded respect everywhere she went. She was known in the office for her sharp wit, bright smile and genuine concern for the needs of both staff and clients.

Imagine my surprise when she called me into her office one day. I was not a part of her team and had only met her once in passing. Therefore, I could not fathom why she needed to see me urgently.

I sheepishly knocked on her open office door. She looked up from the pile of paperwork she was completing and beckoned for me to come in and sit. What she said next surprised me.

She said, "I see something great in you and I want you on my team. There is a position opening up in a few weeks as a business development officer. I want you to apply."

I was stunned. This bold woman with her strong black confidence wanted little ol' me to join her dynamic team. I looked intently at her and asked, "Why me?"

She took off her glasses, looked me directly in the eyes and said, "This world can be a strange and lonely place. We must support each other as black women. I see you going places and want to give you the guidance you need to get to the next level. You are a smart woman and I'd be lucky to have you on the team."

Seems like a fairytale, doesn't it?

It is very rare to hear a business leader of any kind share such encouraging words. Too often, black women in business treat each other like threats instead of allies. This financial services manager thought differently.

I applied for the vacancy, did the interview and got the position. The work was challenging but this lady took me under her wing and became one of my mentors. She still has a prevalent influence on my life to this day.

She taught me four important lessons.

Lesson #1: Do not live in fear.

It is easy to get sidetracked by everything negative happening to the black community. It is also easy to become crippled by fear as you try to make a name for yourself as a black woman in the cutthroat corporate world.

However, fear gets you nowhere. Yes, acknowledging the fear is important; it shows that you feel something and that is something you should never lose. How you respond to this fear, though, is ultimately what matters.

You have to develop the confidence necessary to show that you matter because of your intelligence, skills and experience. Holding back because of your fear will cause you to get left behind. This confidence is developed by:

- Being authentic.
- Demonstrating strong ethics and values.

- Firmly (but respectfully) making your voice heard.
- Going the extra mile.
- Developing genuine relationships with all people regardless of skin color, status or experience.
- Learning to forgive.
- Understanding that you will inevitably have setbacks when you step forward, but you should view them as learning opportunities.

Lesson #2: Accept that not everyone will understand your unique struggles.

We want everyone to understand what it is like being a black woman in the workplace and raising a black child in a racially tense society. If everyone understood, one would think that morality would step in and cause a radical change in how black people are perceived and treated.

Sadly, everyone ***will not*** understand because that is not their experience and they are clouded by their own biases. There is also no real incentive for anyone who is not going through what you are going through to lend a helping hand. Cold as those words may sound, life is almost always easier when the person understands your reality.

But fear not, my sister, be courageous, go out there and demonstrate your merit based on the strength of your character, the quality of your work and the values that you uphold.

Many may not understand your struggle, but you should still have a single-minded focus about shining your light and thriving.

Lesson #3: You must work twice as hard.

We already have two things working against us; we are black and we are women. The Washington Center for Equitable Growth published a paper in July 2018 entitled *Returns in the Labor Market: A Nuanced View of Penalties at the Intersection of Race and Gender* which supports what we already know—black women constantly face a race and gender gap when compared with their counterparts.

It is an unjust system; one that we can only change through establishing a united front across the country. We need more black women to be the decision makers in government and have prominent positions in the places we work. We need to own our own businesses, industries, networks...we need to lead.

For real change to happen, we must be the ones who are setting the rules or the ones having the authority to influence the narrative.

Until then, we are trapped in this reality of having to work twice as hard. However, this does not mean that you should settle for this reality and continue to work in a place where you are afraid to speak up and shine your light. You can take control of your destiny by working towards a game plan where you influence the narrative and level up the playing field.

For example, starting your own business or leading a community initiative, will put you in a place of influence.

Lesson #4: You cannot go through this alone.

Having strong faith in our individual strength as black women can sometimes work against us. We are wired to think that we need to fight for our rights, fight for what we believe and just keep fighting...alone. You cannot keep fighting in silence and expect consistent victories.

You need a community of support, a community that understands that when we fight, we fight together. This community may be a close group of friends who share in your frustrations and provide the advice you need to make the best decision. Another community option is a strong group of like-minded strangers who rally together for a common good. It is good to be a part of both communities.

Search for common causes, build with your black sisters, and be amazed by what you are able to achieve through unity and collaboration.

What does this mean for you?

You may not be fortunate enough to have a black female mentor. However, that does not mean that you cannot keep working towards your vision, become a catalyst of change and find existing networks of black sisters who can give you the support you need.

Establish a support network for black women in your community.

Instead of waiting for something to be done, you can be the black woman who unites your community. Each group of black women in this country and the world faces a unique set of issues depending on where they live and the nuances of their communities.

A black woman in Minnesota will probably not face the same issues as a black woman in Florida. A black woman in London will probably not face the same issues as a black woman in Cape Town.

You have experienced the issues in your community first-hand. There are other black women in your community who are having the same experiences. Find them and create a platform where all of you can provide meaningful support for each other.

One of the ways that you could find these women is by searching for them on social media. For instance, you can type "black women in Florida" on Facebook and find a list of people who fit that description.

When you find them, you could send a message that sounds something like this:

> *Hi! I know this may seem strange, but I live in [insert name of state here] and I'm trying to create a network of black women in our area. The aim of this network is to provide inspiration, motivation and support for black women in our community*

because we're not in this alone. Would you be interested in becoming a part of this network?

You can then create a Facebook group where you can schedule regular online events and group discussions to provide the networking opportunities and support black women crave.

Find existing support communities.

Social media has made it so easy to find online support communities for anything imaginable. Type "Black Women in America" on Facebook and you will find a lot of groups filled with thousands of women who can relate to your experiences. Some examples include:

- Black Women in Corporate America.
- Black Women Support Each Other.
- Back Women Business Owners.
- Black Women Code.

You can do the same on Twitter, Instagram, LinkedIn... basically any social media network. You will find people you can follow or groups you can join. Use social media to do more than scroll through for a good laugh.

Become an active member of a non-profit organization, specifically for black women.

You can volunteer at one (or more) of the many non-profit organizations in America specifically created for black women. Do your research to find one that suits your values and interests and put in the work to make a difference. Some possibilities include:

- Black Women for Wellness.
- Black Women's Blueprint.
- Center for Black Equity.
- National Association for the Advancement of Colored People (NAACP).
- National Black Women's Justice Institute.
- National Congress of Black Women.

The more active you become, the greater your chances of finding a black female mentor who can offer the guidance you need. Waiting for that mentor to pop up at your workplace may leave you stuck in a repetitive cycle of "woulda, coulda, shoulda". That is not what you want.

Be deliberate in how you raise your children.

There is no perfect solution for raising black children in a world where our race tends to be viewed as inferior. We cannot control the actions and thoughts of those around us, and that is terrifying in itself. Additionally, we cannot be there to protect our children every second of the day.

You want your children to be a part of the vision you created in chapter two. Maybe you do not have children of your own, but you have nieces, nephews or young cousins who look up to you. You are a part of the village that raises them.

One of the greatest lessons you can teach them is to not live with a spirit of fear. Instead, the confidence and strength you exude as you work towards your vision should inspire them to do the same. It is about feeding the fire inside these children to be a part of a beautiful vision of change.

My mother always told me that I am special. Those words helped shape my identity because I believed them at my core. They have uplifted my spirit and helped me work towards making an impact on this world.

The children in your circle already know that they are special because of the color of their skin. However, you should help them to see that they are special because of who they are and what they have to offer to the world. Words of affirmation and encouragement provide mental soul food for your children.

Empower your kids by letting them know they are loved, special and are born to make an impact. These positive words will help shape their identity.

The world is challenging but it is your responsibility to help your children to become strong and fearless. They should know that no matter what life throws at them, they can always pick themselves back up and come back with an even clearer sense of the immense value they must add to this world. That is what we need to teach our children. It is tough, but it is necessary.

It also helps to talk with your community of black sisters about the issues you face raising children in this society. Remember that you are not in this fight alone.

Your sisters can provide some helpful tips and inspiration to deal with some of the challenges you face raising your child (or helping to raise the children around you).

Final Thoughts

The racial and gender divide that plagues our society seems to be getting worse rather than better. What are we going to do about it? Are we going to hide and crawl into our safe places? What example does that set for the young black girls and boys we are raising?

We must unite as sisters to not only support each other's visions, but also support the complete dismantling of this nonsensical racial and gender divide. You and I need to be a part of the change, we need to lead, grow and build our own.

I have already begun to find the right networks of black American women for me. It is time for you to do the same.

REFLECTION QUESTIONS

1. How are you going to pave the way towards a brighter future for black women in America?
2. What are some of the unique challenges faced by black women in your immediate community? How can you help solve some of these challenges?
3. Besides social media, are there other ways that you can bring black women in your community together to establish a strong, local sisterhood?
4. Which black non-profit organizations are you going to join?

PART 2

The Leap

"Your world is only as small
as you make it."
~Gabrielle Union

CHAPTER 4

Challenge the Stereotypes

> "Worry about being respected, never worry about being liked because that's the trap."
>
> ~Jada Pinkett Smith

We have two things working against us as black women in America—our skin color and our gender. It is tiring thinking about how our education, wit and fortitude tend to be overlooked because of the innate characteristics we were blessed with.

Someone I know shared an experience she had with black stereotyping in a Facebook post early in 2020. She is an intelligent young woman who has a Bachelor's degree in psychology and a Doctor of Medicine (MD) degree. She also now specializes as a doctor of internal medicine and works as an assistant professor of clinical medicine.

In this Facebook post, she was describing an experience

she had with a COVID-19 patient. Her colleagues had already warned her that he was a difficult patient because he had a medical background and was, therefore, demanding every treatment he knew for COVID-19 (including those that had no longer proven to be effective).

She entered his room, did an examination and discussed the treatment plan with him. He then looked at her and essentially said that she reminded him of a ***black*** female doctor he had met a long time ago who had a good bedside manner and was ***surprisingly smart.***

Compliments are great. However, why emphasize that she was a black female doctor who was surprisingly smart? Why couldn't he just have said that her great bedside manner and intellect reminded him of a doctor he met many years ago?

I do not know if he realized it, but his statement showcased two stereotypes. Firstly, it implied that it is strange to see a ***black female*** doctor. Secondly, it implied that it is even more shocking to see a black female doctor who is smart.

My Experience with Stereotypes

I shared one of my experiences with stereotypes when I described how I felt at my first job in New York in Chapter Two. Sadly, I have had too many of these experiences in different settings.

Two of these experiences stick out in my mind because I felt a sense of betrayal and they moved beyond stereotyping into blatant racism. The first involved the guy I was dating about three years ago.

As a "black man", I expected him to be able to fully understand the struggles I face as a black woman in America. I also believed that he would value and respect me as his partner because he claimed to love me.

There were days when we would get into arguments because we could not see eye-to-eye on issues raised by the Black Lives Matter movement, issues I expected him to completely understand. He could not understand why "black lives matter" was an important message when all lives matter, and blacks seemed to be doing well for themselves in the corporate world and in the sports and entertainment industries.

On top of this, I had clear evidence to show that some of the challenges I was having at work were brought on because of the color of my skin. However, he would insinuate that maybe I was the problem. Maybe I should just, as he put it, "stay in my lane" or "stop causing more trouble".

My explanations were futile. The fact that I was never afraid to speak my mind and stand up as a strong woman in the relationship also added more fuel to the fire.

We were on rocky soil, but he had some amazing qualities that I was looking for in a life partner. He was supportive of my endeavors, loved children and had a steady job.

Imagine my surprise when I approached the door of his

apartment one day and overheard him talking to one of his friends. Here is a breakdown of the conversation. Let's call my ex-boyfriend Jamal and his friend Andre.

"Why are you still with that chick, bro?" asked Andre.

"The sex is good, but I can't stand her talking back to me and getting into this whole women empowerment and Black Lives Matter shit," Jamal replied.

"Good sex is great, bro, but you can't have this nappy hair disrespecting you like that. Who does she think she is? Harriet Tubman?" said Andre.

"The only way I believe we can progress in this society as black people is to play by their rules. If we can't beat them, it's best we just go with the flow," Jamal replied.

"Man, I feel you. You probably need to ditch that girl 'cause she ain't about that life," said Andre.

I could not stand to listen to anymore of the conversation, so I turned around, walked back to my apartment and called him about an hour later to end the relationship. I told him that it did not make sense moving forward since we didn't see eye-to-eye on so many things, but I never told him what I overheard. It did not even take much convincing; we ended the relationship and he wished me all the best.

Damn hypocrite.

I now understand the words Malcolm X uttered back in 1962:

"The most disrespected person in America is the black woman. The most unprotected person in America is the black woman. The most neglected person in America is the black woman."

Malcolm also went on to say that a black man should be willing to lay down his life to support and protect a black woman.

My second experience with blatant stereotyping and racism occurred on a bright summer day about a year and a half ago when I was standing in line at Starbucks. I was there minding my own business when I sensed someone staring at me.

I looked up and my eyes connected with the eyes of an older white woman seated at a table nearby. Her eyes were filled with hatred and disgust. In them, I saw a message of, "You don't belong here and you need to get out."

After I purchased my coffee, I walked over to her and said, "Hi. My name is Erika and I noticed you looking at me a while ago. I just wanted to say that I hope you have a great day."

She was stunned. Instead of thanking me, she looked directly into my eyes and said, "What gives ***you*** the right to talk to me?" She then got up and walked away.

I had done nothing wrong. My only crime, apparently, was being black. How dare a black woman enter a coffee shop to spend her hard-earned money on a nice latte! Black people have no right to enjoy life, to live, to eat, to breathe...who are we to think that we are all a part of one human race?

Leaping Beyond Stereotypes

Chances are that you have experienced stereotypes and racism in some way as a black woman in America. However, the only way that you and I can leap into the game plans we have created for our lives is to look beyond the stereotypes.

We cannot accept that black women are not good enough.

We cannot accept that black women cannot speak their minds and stand up for what is right.

We cannot accept that black women are not allowed to show kindness to strangers.

We cannot accept that black women are only good for breeding children.

Reading the words in this chapter have probably caused you to feel angry. You have every right to be, and we need that anger to transform into initiative. It is time to channel your anger, hurt and pain, as a result of black stereotypes, into taking a giant leap towards accomplishing your game plan.

The quote from Jada Pinkett Smith used at the beginning of this chapter paints a clear picture of the first thing you need to do to take that giant leap—earn respect.

Three truths about earning respect as a black woman:

1. Understand that not everyone is meant to be in your circle.

Stop trying to fit into a mold. Instead, surround yourself with a diverse group of like-minded people from all ethnicities and social backgrounds. Call out the people in your circle the moment you notice they are not standing up for truth, justice and equality.

Respect their perspectives but also paint a clear picture of where they went wrong. If there is not a mindset shift, it is time to let that person go.

2. Speak a consistent message.

People who are consistent in the way they behave and the messages they speak earn the respect of those around them. You cannot stand up for something one day and then forget about it the following day because you are too tired to stand up for what is right.

Therefore, you need to clearly understand who you are and what you stand for. There will be people who look for bad things to say about you, but do not let that deter you. We are not perfect and we will make mistakes.

Nevertheless, you should always strive to consistently show up as a woman of integrity, intellect, poise and dignity. A woman who is not afraid to let her truth be spoken about the injustices of society and who is not afraid to play her part in doing something about them.

3. Never compromise on your morals and values.

The road to success has many paths. Choose the path that aligns with your morals and values. It may be a path filled with rocks, ditches, mud and dirt, but at least you will emerge on the other side with your integrity intact and the respect of those around you. Do not compromise who you are to suit any hidden agendas.

Stereotypes are meant to be challenged.

A stereotype is essentially a prejudiced belief about a group of people. There really is no sound logic for many of the stereotypes that exist in the world today. Your best response to the stereotypes about black women is to ***prove them wrong***.

Sure, there will be days when you meet someone like the lady in Starbucks whose stereotyping causes your blood to boil. However, undoing decades of falsehood that have been ingrained into someone's psyche is difficult, especially if it is just someone you see in passing.

Your actions are the only things that you can control and the best way to act is to build up your reputation as a pillar of strength in your community. Let people hear about you on the news for the good you do and the giant leaps you have taken to achieve success not only for yourself, but for your black sisters and brothers.

Change the world through what you do. Challenge stereotypes by being the black woman who is not any of those negative things spouted by those with prejudices. Encourage your sisterhoods to do the same, and that is how you will start seeing growth and change in this messed up world.

Do not stop speaking up, do not stop leading, do not stop learning and keep moving forward with style and dignity.

Leap Beyond Fear

Fear may be one of the reasons you feel trapped by the stereotypes imposed on you by the world. You may be afraid of losing your job or your life if you speak up. There may also be a fear of the repercussions of the positive actions you take towards success on your family and friends. Your fear could also be as simple as not wanting to hear the word, "no".

These are very real fears; fears that are often difficult to address. The reality is that the best way to really deal with fear is to find a limitless level of inner strength and fortitude. It is really a mental battle you face with yourself. Here are some tips that you can use to win the battle.

Reframe Fear

Use fear as your motivation to act. I am not saying that you should act on impulse and make irrational decisions. Instead, use your fear to create a plan and execute it.

For instance, you have probably been concerned about the lack of representation of black people at your workplace but have been too afraid to speak up. Channel your fear into creating a plan to approach one of the company's leaders with a proposal for increasing black representation.

Do your research on companies that have made similar changes and clearly explain how the company you work for can benefit. Show them the profit drivers and cultural benefits from having a more diverse workforce.

Let Go of Security

Chasing security has probably caused you to make decisions that jeopardize the fulfillment of your vision. You cannot make a giant leap if you don't value courage over security. Bold moves are necessary for you to walk into your purpose. Remember that you are not trying to contribute to the wealth of the graveyard!

Listen to Your Fears

I discussed the importance of changing your self-talk in Chapter One. The strategies I mentioned are applicable to listening to and dealing with your fears. Listen to what your fear is telling you about who you are and what you can and cannot do. Challenge the thoughts by developing a positive narrative.

For instance, you may be afraid to leave your job and start your own business because you do not think you have what it takes. Your fear is telling you that you are incapable. Change your thinking by saying, "I can start a business that allows me to pursue my passions. I will follow the steps and strategies I have outlined in my game plan to make it happen. I am capable and I'm going to get it done."

REFLECTION QUESTIONS

1. What stereotypes have you experienced as a black woman in America?
2. Have you made these stereotypes become your narrative? How can you challenge them?
3. What do you need to change about your actions so that you can earn the respect of those around you?
4. What one fear can you overcome today?

CHAPTER 5

Define Your Personal Brand

> "The only person you should compare yourself to is the person you used to be in the past."
>
> ~Taraji Henson

THE HOLIDAYS WERE quickly approaching and I was buried deep in year-end reports. This was one of those evenings where I was alone in the office since everyone else had already left for the day.

I enjoyed the peace of the quiet office. Moments like these helped me perform at my best. My apartment was only a few blocks away and I never felt afraid of walking home alone late at night.

Until tonight.

It was about 10:00 pm that Friday evening when I exited the office building. It was chilly so I was fiddling with my scarf to ensure that my neck was completely covered.

That's when I heard him.

His short, heavy breathing pierced the night sky. The streets were busy, but somehow his breathing seemed louder than everything else. I turned my head and our eyes connected.

He seemed like a ghost from my past, a memory I had hoped to forget.

We stood in silence, staring intently at each other. Everything happening around us seemed to freeze in that moment. I felt myself being enamored by his chocolate brown skin, hazel brown eyes and piercing stare that always made me feel like he was looking right through me.

I started walking towards him, but then he started to back away. I started running and he turned and ran into the street. A car was approaching at break-neck speed and hit his muscular frame.

"*No!*" I screamed as I knelt on the pavement and wept.

When I looked up, there was a group of people staring at me. "What are you guys staring at? Didn't you see that car hit that guy?" I asked.

"What're you talking about? Are you okay? Do you need to go to the hospital?" asked a lady who was trying to help me stand up.

I looked back at the street where I saw the car and my love collide. There was nothing there. It was like he had vanished. There were no traces of blood and no sign of the car.

There was now a group of about six people surrounding me, eyes filled with concern. "I thought I saw my boyfriend get hit by a car..." I breathed.

"Nah, nothing like that happened. Maybe you should go home and rest," said one of the guys in the crowd.

That's when it dawned on me. I was reliving a version of the night when the love of my life was killed in a tragic accident. Probably it was the hurt I felt from being alone this holiday season or working late every night was taking its toll.

I had been visited by a ghost from my past. All I could do now was run from the overwhelming hurt that ravaged my heart and hide myself away from the embarrassment of looking like a fool on a New York City street.

So, that is what I did. I broke free from the small crowd of concerned onlookers and ran for three blocks back to my apartment.

It was time to reflect and move forward.

In Chapter One, I discussed the importance of cleaning out the cobwebs in your mind, cobwebs formed from the pain of those who you felt have wronged you. However, we did not look at how to let go of the person you were in the past to make room for the person you are meant to be today.

This reality struck me that night as I reflected on my hallucination. I had spent the past year and a half preparing myself to make a giant leap towards my vision. Little did I realize that there were some elements of my past I was holding on to too tightly.

My boyfriend was my knight in shining armor. I met him a few months after I had broken up with the hypocrite I described in Chapter Four. That hypocrite had caused me to become unnecessarily defensive and always made me feel like I had to prove my worth; add that to the pressure of having to prove myself as a black woman at work and amongst my peers, and I was drowning.

This chocolate hunk of a man came and helped me understand my worth. But when he died, my world was shattered. I began to shrink back into my shell and put on my defenses in an attempt to deal with this dark, lonely world.

I thought that I was doing okay. However, that night on those cold New York City streets proved I was not. I needed to think carefully about who I needed to become so that the personal brand I was portraying to the world was actually a true reflection of who I am. I ***know*** I was not that terrified, defensive girl who ran away and cried that night.

Defining My Personal Brand

Your personal brand is essentially the image you portray to the world about who you are and what you stand for. I have been alluding to it throughout the past four chapters, but I want to dive into it a bit more.

I believe that my personal brand should not be a façade I present to the world. I wanted my personal brand to portray how I felt while in my beautiful relationship with my knight in shining armor. I wanted my personal brand to be authentic.

So, it was a matter of deciding within myself ***how*** I would develop the strength to exude that confidence, authenticity, and self-worth as well as ***how*** I would portray this to the world. The former relied heavily on understanding my core philosophy. The latter relied on understanding how my core philosophy aligned with my meaningful work and the value I add to the world.

My Core Philosophy

I had to dig deep to truly understand ***who*** I really am. Am I a woman who allows herself to be defined by the people in her life? Am I a woman who compares herself to others and hides in her shell?

Of course, I knew that my answers to those questions would always be a resounding, "No!" But why didn't I believe that deep down?

I had to now be deliberate about crafting my narrative for who I am and why I am not the person I used to be. I put pen to paper and decided that this would be the core philosophy that defined my life.

> *I, Erika Rae Bailey, am a woman who has experienced a lot of hurt in her lifetime. I accept that this hurt forms an important part of my story and*

> *is something that I should not be ashamed of. I believe that I can make a difference in this world through my love for finance and I can create the future I desire through hard work, discipline and going after the right opportunities. I can (and I will) be a black woman of influence who makes a difference in this world.*

Remember the vision board I created way back in Chapter Two? Well, I hired a graphic designer to create an artistic representation of my core philosophy. I framed it and placed it directly beside my vision board as a visual reminder of this commitment I had made to myself.

It is not about who I ***was*** and the damage that may have been a part of my life. Instead, it is about how I can use my story to change my life and the lives of many other people in this world.

My Meaningful Work

My hallucination made me feel as though I had forgotten my vision board. I had to look back at it and make the connection between my core philosophy and the work I needed to do.

I would only be able to use my love for finance to change the world if I create that financial literacy program for kids and start the Melona Financial Group. Pushing towards this vision, however, meant that I needed to stop running from my past.

You see, I was becoming a workaholic to distract myself from my hurt. Therefore, my focus was not where it needed to be. It was now time to embrace my past as a part of my story and use it as further motivation to step forward into my meaningful work.

The Value I Bring to the Table

I am confident in my abilities and my strength as a black woman. However, there are too many instances where I allow what others do and say to cause me to question my value. I constantly have to remind myself daily that I am enough and my skills and intellect help me add value to the world.

Of course, this does not mean that I think of myself as better than anyone else. It is more about not comparing myself to others and instead comparing who I have become with who I was in the past. I need to value my progress and look forward to making even greater strides as I mature.

My Personal Brand Statement

It was then important for me to coalesce these thoughts into one defining statement. Oftentimes, we limit personal brand statements to defining the way we work. I wanted it to be more than that and felt that my personal brand statement should define who I am at my core and then how that translates into the positive contribution I can make to the world.

Here's what I came up with.

I, Erika Rae Bailey, am defined by the steps I take to be better than who I was in the past and how I use my skills as a finance professional to both develop a financial literacy program for kids across America and become a leader of a respected finance corporation.

What is your personal brand statement?

How you perceive yourself is important for defining who you will become. You will not be able to boldly take the leap towards your vision if you are not 100 percent clear about who you are and how your past has shaped you.

This process is not simple. As my story revealed, there will be times when your past comes back and surprises you. You will not be strong and confident all the time; you'll have your moments of weakness. However, keeping that personal brand statement ringing in your ears increases your chances of quickly regaining focus.

Now, I do not want your personal brand statement to be a replica of mine. For instance, there may be a particular negative event in your life that has helped shape who you are and how you perceive yourself.

Call out that event while writing your core philosophy. Make it very clear that you are better than what happened and believe strongly in your ability to carry out your meaningful work. Articulate clearly how you can make a difference in this world and the value you have to offer.

Once you have done that, frame it and mount it on your wall. The best place to put it is beside your vision board so that you are constantly reminded of both your vision and personal brand statement each day. You should aim to read it at least twice per day, maybe first thing in the morning and right before you go to bed. This will help you to imprint your personal brand statement deep into your subconscious mind.

Use your personal brand statement as a constant reminder of what you need to do to take the leap.

Live with a heart of gratitude.

Ultimately, your ability to thrive as you leap into the unknown depends heavily on your ability to stop comparing yourself to others. That is why your personal brand statement is so important; it helps you identify key things that make you unique and helps you understand the value you bring to the world. Remember that.

Here are some tips that you can try to live with a heart of gratitude if you are struggling with comparing yourself to others.

View each day as a gift.

Gratitude begins by viewing each day as a blessing. Each day brings with it the responsibility to use your skills to effect meaningful change. Comparing yourself to others destroys this precious gift each day brings.

Perspective makes a huge difference.

This point goes back to looking carefully at how you think. Why dwell on the negatives in life? You can accomplish so much more if you choose to view life through a positive lens.

Granted, it is not about having your head in the clouds, thinking that everything is fine and dandy. It is more about training your mind to stop beating yourself up and stop harping on everything that is wrong with your situation.

It is about viewing failures and setbacks as learning opportunities.

Focus on the beauty in what you already have.

Sure, you want a better life filled with everything you have ever dreamed about. That does not mean that you cannot find the beauty in what you already have and appreciate it. If you were to review your life, you would realize that you have achieved far more than you have given yourself credit for.

REFLECTION QUESTIONS

1. How has your past caused you to shape the wrong image of yourself?
2. What steps will you take to stop comparing yourself to others?
3. How can you develop a heart of gratitude?
4. What is your personal brand statement?

CHAPTER 6

From Passion to Profit

> "Don't ever let what a man brings to the table be all you have to eat."
>
> ~Phylicia Rashad

I FERVENTLY BELIEVE THAT proper financial management is the key to success. Sure, qualities such as self-belief and hard work are important. However, what you do with the money you have can mean the difference between leaping into prosperity or disaster.

I have experienced natural and man-made disasters in my lifetime ranging from hurricanes and snowstorms to pandemics, recessions, and the collapse of the financial markets. These challenges set back plans and goals. You may have plans to start a business, go on a vacation, take on a huge client, step into that dream life... the list goes on.

But then all those plans seem to go down the drain because of the unexpected, and one thing I can guarantee is that the unexpected will always come along at some point in your journey.

Those who thrive during and after any major crisis are those who have a grip on their finances and know how to transform their passions into profit.

As a finance professional, I would not encourage you to glow without providing some clarity on how you can manage your personal finances for lasting success. You cannot confidently take the leap into your vision without honing your ability to manage your finances.

I am by no means suggesting that doing this is easy or that I have millions tucked away in a secret account. To be honest, I have come to realize, throughout my life, that everyone's journey to financial freedom is different.

Some people may get the right opportunities and be able to manage their personal finances well enough to become millionaires by the age of 30. On the other hand, it may take me a longer time to achieve the same result even if I follow the same strategies as my counterparts who are better off. I have learnt to focus on my journey and how I am able to manage my finances with each new wave of challenges unique to my life.

The Highs and Lows

Describing my experience growing up is a bit tricky. I mentioned in Chapter One that I was raised by a single mother. All my basic needs were provided for and my mother ensured that I had everything I needed (and more) for my education.

However, doing this was often at the expense of her own needs. I remember the days when all we were living on was my grandmother's pension (about $2000 per month) because my mother could not find a job. My dad would also send about $200 monthly to cover my basic needs, and my mother would give me about half of it each month as lunch money while she kept the rest to cover the basic expenses of the house.

One day, I asked my mother if I could get all the money dad sent for me because I had plans to save towards a future goal. She did not hesitate to agree with my request despite needing the money to take care of the household. So, that $2000 from my grandmother's pension was used to buy groceries, pay the bills and purchase medication for both my mother and grandmother.

It was not that I did not care about what my mother was going through. I did. But I also wanted to avoid getting myself into the same situation; I wanted to grow into a woman who was financially stable so that I could give my mother and grandmother the lives they deserve. My request was my foray into understanding how to manage money.

Like most other university students, I had to apply for a student loan to pay my tuition. My dad did not even want me to go to university. He felt that I should go straight into the working world and find my own way to get the money I needed to pursue higher education.

My strong, beautiful mother was adamant that I had to go to university. She could not afford to send me, but she knew I had to go and I had to live on campus. That then led to the discussion of how my dorm fees would be paid.

I remember being in the final semester of my first year, completely clueless about how my dorm fees would be paid. I looked at the bank account that had all my savings from my childhood and it was enough to cover that semester. So, I told my mom that everything would be okay and that I would cover the cost.

However, I felt sad about it for some reason. I had asked my boyfriend at the time to go with me to the bank; I vividly remember crying on his shoulder on the way back home. I think they were tears of frustration.

Frustration about trying so hard yet not being able to use the money for its intended purpose.

Frustration about not having the life I desired.

Frustration that I will have to start out in my career saddled with $40,000 in student loan debt.

Frustration about not wanting to end up in a predicament like my mother who had a failed company, a mountain of debt and was barely making ends meet.

These frustrations represented a low point for me. I vowed that I would make the best possible financial decisions I could once I started working.

In Chapter One, I explained that I studied math with education at university and my career began as a math teacher, a job I hated. It was difficult for me to achieve my financial goals on a teacher's salary, plus pay off my student loan. I lived with my mom, so I was able to save money on rent and utilities. I was also making a deliberate attempt to save 20 percent of whatever I earned, a habit I had developed as a teenager.

I wanted to achieve financial success but would always get caught in two traps:

- Tapping into my savings to meet immediate needs.
- Skipping a few months here and there because I wanted to spend some money on myself.

I would get into a cycle of saving (and even investing in stocks) until my money got to a certain level and then tapping into it to meet important needs. This cycle, coupled with the observations I made of my mom's lack of financial prudence, taught me three valuable lessons about managing personal finances.

Lesson #1: Save to invest.

Keeping money in a bank account I could easily access was not a great way to resist dipping into the funds. You see, all it takes is one dive into the money pool and you find yourself spending more than necessary. Add that to the fact that the low interest rates mean that the money is not earning real interest and saving for the sake of saving truly becomes pointless.

I have realized that the best approach to saving is to save with an investment goal in mind. What that means is saving towards an amount that you can then use to invest in a diverse portfolio of stocks, bonds, real estate and other assets. Either that or using that amount to invest in a well-thought-out business venture.

Therefore, I have started to set $1,000-goals for myself. Whenever my savings hit that amount, I channel my funds into my investment portfolio. I am also growing my investment portfolio to an amount that I can use as seed money for the Melona Financial Group.

Lesson #2: A rainy-day fund matters.

A savings account does have relevance beyond accumulating funds that can be used for investments. This is a fact I have only begun to appreciate more recently. It is important to have a separate savings account that acts as your rainy-day fund.

It is the account in which you set aside at least 5 to 10 percent of your salary each month. You should continue adding to your rainy-day fund until you have at least 6 months' equivalent of your monthly expenses saved up. I personally shoot for 9 months' equivalent of my monthly expenses.

This money should only be used for ***emergencies.*** Its purpose is not to fund that pair of Louis Vuitton heels you have been eyeing for the past three months.

Lesson #3: The financial preliminaries are important.

Most finance professionals recommend that their clients have three financial preliminaries prior to embarking on any investment. These financial preliminaries are:

- Cash reserves (the rainy-day fund).
- Life insurance (it helps even more if you get a life insurance policy with an investment component you can access throughout your life; property insurance is also a plus).
- Health insurance.

Having these financial preliminaries decreases the likelihood of you tapping into your investments to cover emergencies.

I think I had an *"Aha!"* moment when I realized this truth. Sure, I had been investing in the stock market and some unit trust instruments. However, I had to sell ***everything*** when I needed to cover some expenses because I did not have any cash reserves and did not have any health insurance.

Life insurance and health insurance are expensive; no doubt about that. However, the benefits they provide at the times they are needed surpass the monthly payments you have to make, especially if you have dependents. It is all about working the monthly payments into your budget.

How can you structure your finances to prepare for the leap?

You are a strong, intelligent and talented black woman who is poised for greatness. I want you to step into your own financial freedom without the need to lean on anyone for financial support.

Having a firm financial foundation in place will help you to feel more confident and open you up to more opportunities; your power strut will be there for all to see! It is a great position to be in. It will not be an easy road, but you will be grateful for the experience in the long term.

You've got this!

In fact, mastering personal finances will help you better understand how to manage your business' finances if becoming an entrepreneur is a part of your vision. It is also a lesson that you could teach to your children which, undoubtedly, will set them up for a far brighter future.

Therefore, I believe you should bide in a state of financial security by following the steps of the B-I-D-E personal finance structure.

B- Budget.

I am still not great at this, but I know that budgeting is important for developing a habit of financial prudence. My monthly budget is structured like an income and expenditure statement, with income on the left and expenses on the right. In fact, you can view it as a balance sheet that you would use for a company.

Here is an example. Please note that these are just figures I made up and do not necessarily represent my actual income and expenses.

Income	**Expenditure**
Net Salary - $3,500	Utilities + Phone Bill - $375
Other - $500	Rent - $1000
	Taxes - $500
	Groceries - $250
	Car Payments + Gas- $350 + $60
	Life Insurance - $55
	Health Insurance - $30*
	Car Insurance - $30*
	Entertainment (Including Eating Out) - $150
	Miscellaneous - $1,200**
TOTAL: $4,000	**TOTAL: $4,000**

* Although I pay my health insurance and car insurance annually, I divide those payments into monthly installments so that I am saving towards the annual figure. That way, I do not have to hurriedly search for the funds when the annual payment arises.

** I actually work out the miscellaneous figure first when doing my budget because it is important to develop the habit of paying yourself first. This figure is always 30 percent of my total income (10 percent for the rainy-day fund and 20 percent for investment).

A monthly budget helps you develop the discipline of spending your money wisely. In fact, most banks now have mobile apps that allow you to prepare a budget and track your spending based on that budget. The tracking feature is important for ensuring that you are sticking within the parameters you have established.

I- Identify the right debt for your budget.

Debt is often the primary culprit for poor financial management. We often take on more debt than we can afford and end up in a tailspin trying to figure out how we are going to repay it. My mantra is to only take on debt where I can clearly see the funds I will be using to repay it.

You should also take on what is termed "good debt". An example of good debt is taking out a mortgage to purchase a rental property from which you earn monthly income. You now have a lucrative asset that can be used to improve your monthly cash flow position.

Remaining on the topic of debt management, one of my mother's financial pitfalls was taking on debt based on money that was promised to her; I vowed never to make the same mistake. Therefore, I only make debt decisions based on money I have and my current income.

There are several tools you can use to identify the right

credit cards and loans for your financial needs. Websites like *Nerd Wallet*, offer a wealth of advice on how to choose debt wisely. Check these sites out.

D- Diversify your income.

You will notice that I have a line item in my budget called “Other”. That is the label I use for any money I earn outside of my 9 to 5.

The best way to build financial independence is to have multiple sources of income. Numerous studies have shown that the average millionaire has seven streams of income.

Depending on your full-time job alone is risky, especially if you want to leap into your vision sooner rather than later. Multiple income sources add to your personal profit and provide you with strong fundamentals to deal with any fluctuations in the job market.

One of the strategies you can use to diversify your income is to make money online. Starting an online business is relatively low-cost, but it does provide the vehicle to scale rapidly because you can sell your services to a global marketplace.

Some of the most popular online business models include affiliate marketing, fulfillment by Amazon (FBA), eCommerce, coaching, copywriting, blogging, dropshipping, and social media marketing agencies.

This is not the book for discussing how these business models work. However, there is a plethora of resources available online that can steer you in the right direction. Do your research and find what works for you.

E- Evaluate your progress.

I believe in the power of feedback and reflection. Evaluation should always be a part of any financial steps you take. Here are some questions you can ask to test whether you are progressing in the right direction:

1. Are my expenses less than 70 percent of my income? I would say that it is ideal to work towards having your expenses being 50 percent of your income. That definitely means that you will need to find additional income sources.
2. Does the amount of money in my rainy-day fund represent at least six months of my monthly expenses?
3. What rate of return am I able to achieve on my investments? How can I improve this rate of return?

REFLECTION QUESTIONS

1. What changes do you need to make to your existing budget so that you are not overspending?
2. How can you diversify your income?
3. If you want to become an entrepreneur, how much money do you need to save to get your business off the ground?
4. How much money do you presently have in your rainy-day fund?

Get FREE Books Before They Are Released!

Join the Insider's Club and we will email you **FREE** copies of new books before we publish them.

You may ask, why would we give away our books for **FREE**?

Well, our ***VIP Insider Club Members*** help us greatly with fine-tuning a book before it goes on general release.

We value any feedback and input provided, whenever it is needed. We have some of the best editors in the business, but now and then, our eagle-eyed Insider Club Members will spot something that could do with a little tweaking…thanks in advance!

We publish non-fiction and fiction books, from business, self-help and health books to children's stories and romance novels.

Click (or tap) below to JOIN the exclusive **VIP Insider Club Members** and start receiving FREE Books before they are published.

Click here:
https://www.mangobroom.com/insiders-club/

PART 3

Own Your Power

"Let go of fear and
shame of judgement. Be
authentic."
~Dorinda Walker

CHAPTER 7

Glow in Your Boss Suit

> "The business of being a black woman is an act of courage."
>
> -Michaela Angela Davis

IT TAKES COURAGE to step boldly into business as a black woman. Heck, it takes courage to even be a black woman in America. Period.

The thought of starting a business in America as a black woman can make some people cringe. One of the many reasons for this is lack of funding. Business funding for female entrepreneurs is limited while such funding for African American female entrepreneurs is virtually non-existent. It is not uncommon to feel like we have been given a basket to carry water.

Yet, we still ***rise to the occasion.***

American Express commissioned a report in 2018 about the state of women-owned businesses in the US. The report revealed that there were 2.4 million female-owned African American businesses. In fact, African

American women were the only women who had more businesses in 2018 than their male counterparts.

When we commit to something, we crush the hell out of it!

Mediocrity is not a part of our DNA.

Let me make one thing clear before I continue—not everyone is destined to be an entrepreneur. Some people are not wired for the rigors of entrepreneurship and may find themselves more suited to the role of an employee, and vice versa. Both the entrepreneur and the employee play an important part in business growth and development.

With that said, I still think entrepreneurship is a good path to take if you want to achieve independence and financial freedom. It is risky, for sure. However, you can reap great rewards when you get it right.

On the other hand, if you approach entrepreneurship without due care, it can become a huge burden to carry and you risk losing all you have. Let us look at what took place when my friend jumped into full-time entrepreneurship too quickly.

Amani's Story

(Please note that Amani is not my friend's real name. I have used a pseudonym for the sake of anonymity.)

I met Amani when I started working at a finance firm in downtown New York City. We were cubicle buddies and shared a cubicle in the cramped office.

Amani is intelligent, vivacious, caring and a respected finance professional. She loved working at this small finance firm but felt that she could do so much more. She wanted to create a venture capital firm to fund businesses owned by African American women.

Her business idea was brilliant. There was not any logical reason for things to go wrong. The market was there and her finance acumen would help her make wise investment decisions.

We often spoke about her idea when we would hang out on the weekends. She even wanted me to be a member of the board. I obliged but told her that she needed to be very strategic in her approach to this business.

I remember going for a run with her in Central Park one Saturday evening. It was the middle of summer, so it was sunny and the temperature was just right. We were taking a break and stretching our legs on one of the benches.

She said, "Erika, I'm so excited about this business idea! There are so many women like us who need this financial support to get their businesses off the ground. A lot of them are depending on these businesses to finance their family's needs. I want to work with these women who have a fire in their belly to make their businesses work and inspire positive change in this crazy world."

"That sounds great, Amani! I'm really proud of you! I want to do something similar with the Melona Financial Group but I'll probably focus on a different section of the market. Remember though that you need to think carefully about how you're going to approach this business," I replied.

It seemed like she had not heard a word I said because she was now speaking in an excited flurry, gushing with enthusiasm about the potential of this lucrative business idea. All I could do was nod my head and smile while she spoke.

She did not listen to my advice and ended up making three critical mistakes. Granted, her business is starting to grow, but she could have gotten to this stage more quickly if she had been more strategic about how she started it.

Here are the mistakes.

She did not get a mentor.

Venture capitalism was something new to Amani. Sure, she had been a financial advisor for about two years and had a bachelor's degree in finance. But her experience and credentials did not provide the depth of knowledge she needed to master the venture capitalist industry right out the gates.

Amani had been planning this business for about a year but never once sought the advice of someone in the field. Probably she was afraid of rejection or was a tad overconfident in her abilities. Whatever the reason, she began to realize the importance of a mentor about a month into the business.

There was no business plan.

Amani was not short on passion, drive and determination. She knew what she wanted to do with this business and the people she would partner with to get there.

Most of the funds she was using to finance the venture capital firm came from a sudden windfall of cash she received from her dad's life insurance policy after he passed. Thankfully, she also had a strong circle of friends who were willing to chip in and had so much confidence in her that they did not ask her for a business plan.

Big mistake. A business plan acts as a roadmap for the development of a successful business. Amani already had a clear vision in her head of what the business would become. However, she did not use a business plan to carefully plan the strategy she would use to get there.

Writing a business plan also forces you to think of things that you may not have thought about. I would advise anyone hoping to start a business to write a business plan because it provides you with a holistic overview of your business strategy and a better understanding of your business model.

She tried to be a jack-of-all-trades.

The thing with being a jack-of-all-trades is that you will be a master of none. I appreciate the fact that a lot of black female entrepreneurs who are just beginning their entrepreneurial journeys have neither the finances nor the wherewithal to get the expert help they need.

Therefore, they end up filling all possible roles within the business from marketing manager to financial controller and customer service representative.

Amani wanted to keep as much of the wealth she had acquired as she could to serve as seed money for the businesses in which her company would invest. That meant that she took on too many roles within the company. This eventually led to incomplete tasks, unhappy entrepreneurs and Amani's burnout within about twelve months of starting the business.

What should you do if you want to glow in your boss suit?

Starting a business may have been a part of the vision you outlined in Chapter Two. That's great! However, I do not want you to jump into entrepreneurship without laying the right foundation to give your business the best chance of success. Let your passion motivate you, but do not allow it to force you to make uninformed decisions.

I have been fortunate enough to serve on the boards of five start-up businesses. Three of them are growing rapidly and have now smashed through the $10m per year turnover level. They are also likely to double these figures in the next 12 months.

The other two are struggling to get past the $500k per

year in revenue because they generally do the opposite of what more successful companies are doing.

Taking the blueprint of the three top-performing companies, let us look at some of the best practices for starting and growing a successful business.

Create a Business Plan

You believe in your idea and know that it can work. There may even be people around you who support the idea and who are encouraging you to make it happen. A business plan helps you map out the idea on paper so that you can create the right business strategy.

It helps you to see around the corner before you get there. You also get to double-check any assumptions and stress test your financial modeling.

This is not the book for going into the details of a business plan. Nevertheless, I will list the sections that you should include in your business plan and encourage you to do further research. I will also encourage you to hire a business plan writer if you need additional support for getting it right.

Sections of the Business Plan:

1. Executive Summary.
2. Company Description.
3. Market Analysis.
4. Competitive Analysis. *
5. Management and Organization.

6. Products and Services.
7. Marketing and Sales Strategy.
8. Financial Projections.

*Novice entrepreneurs sometimes forget to thoroughly assess their competitors. It is an important step to consider because it will help you truly understand your unique selling position (USP).

Start small.

Writing a business plan can be overwhelming. You may have a big idea but no real clue about how to get there. Instead of trying to do everything at once, start small.

You can build your business in stages rather than attempt everything in one go. All you need is a minimally viable product and enough capital to get off the ground.

Take PetitSquares for example. The founder, Monique Farquharson, started the company with what she calls "petit poppers", small sachets of matcha green tea from Japan. Ultimately, she wants to create a matcha café where people can experience all possible applications of matcha in various cuisines.

Monique did not go head-first into the café idea. Instead, she has taken the time to get to know her product well and build an audience using her petit poppers. She probably has one stage of growth left before she ultimately achieves her dream of owning a matcha café.

Decide when in the business cycle you will need additional funding.

I believe in bootstrapping as much as you can to get your business off the ground. Funding should only be sought when you are ready to take the business to the next level and have already established a track-record of success.

However, this does not mean that fresh-out-of-the-box ideas are not able to get the funds they need without having a track-record; it is just that my approach is to test the waters first and put my best foot forward when approaching outside investors. I truly believe this creates the best chance of success because investors will clearly see that you are committed and have put some "skin in the game".

Here is a list of some venture capital firms that fund black female founders (BFFs). You can research these companies and include them in your future funding plans.

- Backstage Capital.
- Cross Culture Ventures.
- New Voices Fund.
- Essence Ventures.
- Kapor Capital.
- The Helm.
- BBG Ventures.

Hire a team.

You will quickly become overwhelmed if you try to do everything alone. Budgetary restrictions may prevent you from hiring full-time staff. However, you can hire remote workers on an as-needed basis to complete many fundamental business tasks.

Upwork is a great platform to use for hiring talented and experienced remote workers. You can use *Upwork* to hire a/an:

- Social media manager.
- Marketing manager.
- Customer service agent.
- Virtual assistant.
- Accountant.
- Content writer for newsletters, blog posts and lead magnets.
- Website designer and developer.

Fiverr is another good platform to consider if you want to hire a graphic designer at affordable rates. I use this platform to meet all my graphic design and logo creation needs.

You will typically find freelancers on these sites who are located in countries with a lower median salary. Therefore, you can benefit from hiring high-quality staff for far less than it would cost if you were hiring someone based in the USA.

Mentors and Masterminds

We often think that a mentor has to be someone who is well-known. Not everyone can have Oprah Winfrey or Angela Beton as a mentor. Therefore, your strategy for finding a mentor who will help you along your journey should center on establishing relationships with people in various mentorship networks and business chambers.

Here are some mentorship networks you can consider:

- Code 2040.
- NewME.
- Code Fever.
- The Black upStart.

You can also find mentors by joining online forums and groups. I have used Facebook groups to gain a lot of knowledge and insights. There is always someone in these groups who is two or three steps ahead of you in certain subjects and would be happy to guide you towards making better decisions based on their experiences.

Do not forget your local mentor—that person down the road with her mom-and-pop store. These owners are some of the best teachers and mentors out there because they are involved in all aspects of running their business on a day-to-day basis. Nothing beats the experience of being on the front line.

I find mom-and-pop store owners to be very welcoming to new entrepreneurs. They love to share their business insights and stories. If you humbly take the lessons on board, you will undoubtedly improve the probability of making your business a massive success.

There is an important point I should mention about mentorship though. It is not a one-way street. Oftentimes, we enter mentorship opportunities expecting to take everything possible from our mentors and give nothing in return.

Suggest ways that you can support your mentor in areas of weakness. For instance, your mentor may not be technologically savvy, but you quickly adapt to any technological advancement. Help her out!

Understand that it will not be an easy road.

Entrepreneurship is not a get rich quick scheme. It will probably take months (maybe even years) for your business to even break-even. Be prepared for the challenges, many of which will be unexpected.

Understanding the reality of entrepreneurship does not mean that you should enter this world with great trepidation. It can be a really fun journey where you get to meet new people, discover your best self and live out your passion. It is an exciting thought to know that you are making your own little impact on the world.

Just be mindful of the mental and financial toll it will take and decide that you will remain committed to the cause even when the road is rough. Finally, remember to enjoy the journey. Your growth will be like the chrysalis that turns into a butterfly.

REFLECTION QUESTIONS

1. You have an idea that you have been carrying around for years. Go ahead and take action. Start today with writing one section of your business plan. I find that entrepreneurs enjoy writing about their "Products and Services" first. Why not start there?
2. Is there anything mentioned in this chapter that you had not previously considered when thinking about your business idea?
3. What makes your business unique?
4. Have you considered starting a micro business with a Minimum Viable Product (MVP)? You may want to start a herbal tea business with 100 different flavors. Why not start with one flavor and start selling it right away?
5. When are you going to apply for funding and what will you be using those funds to do?
6. You may not want to start a business. Do you know someone who does? How can you use what you have learnt in this chapter to help that person?

CHAPTER 8

Be Courageous

> "Don't underestimate the importance you can have because history has shown us that courage can be contagious and hope can take on a life of its own."
>
> ~Michelle Obama

I WAS SICK TO my stomach. Hundreds of people were waiting on me to walk onto the stage and present an awe-inspiring speech.

The spotlight was shining brightly on where I was supposed to stand on the stage. The backstage crew was prodding me to take the steps towards my position.

Me. The girl with the huge afro and brown skin. A woman who had spent her entire life working hard to prove herself to the world. People wanted to hear ***me*** speak.

The applause had stopped while everyone waited with bated breath for me to walk onto the stage. The huge red curtains that hung from the ceiling reminded me of the type of curtains you would see at a large theatre.

This was my debut, my moment to shine. I began walking onto the stage, my heels clicking against the hardwood floors. The applause resumed as I stepped onto the podium, took a deep breath and said, "I have a story to share."

It was not a story of abuse or immense struggle. Instead, it was a story of how I survived corporate America as a black woman. The audience I was speaking to was filled with strong, beautiful black women hoping to learn from the nuggets of wisdom I had to share.

With trembling hands and a shaky voice, I began my speech. The more I spoke, the more confidence I developed. I started walking across the stage, giving jokes, asking the audience questions. I was on fire!

The fear that was initially holding me back became a distant memory. I was now walking in my unique stride and the audience was loving it. My speech ended to a rousing round of applause and standing ovation. I had done what I thought I could not.

This is not a chapter about public speaking. However, I wanted you to get this image in your head of me walking onto that stage. You see, in order to glow, you have to be courageous enough to take the first step.

You will be under a lot of pressure to excel. A lot of people are counting on you to glow in your unique light—your family, friends and community of black sisters. You have two choices; you can either run for the hills or step into the spotlight. Do you have the courage to choose the latter?

Courage is not the absence of fear. In Chapter Four, I encouraged you to leap beyond your fear and one of the strategies for doing that is to listen to your fears. Courage does not mean you are running away from your fears. Instead, you are choosing to acknowledge them and reframe them so that you can take that bold step forward.

The real question is, "How can you develop the courage necessary to step into your destiny?"

My Courage Formula

I have come back to this topic of fear and the courage you will need to overcome it because fear will be an ever-present force in your life. No matter how strong and self-assured you are, there will be moments when fear can seem crippling, especially when you are about to own your power and step into a new opportunity.

If I am being truly honest, I have not completely shaken the fear I feel in moments when I feel like an imposter. I often struggle with Imposter Syndrome as I accomplish the seemingly impossible as a black woman in a racially divided world.

Dr. Valerie Young wrote a book entitled *The Secret Thoughts of Successful Women: Why Capable People Suffer From the Imposter Syndrome and How to Thrive in Spite of It* where she describes five types of Imposter Syndrome:

- The Perfectionist.
- The Superwoman.
- The Natural Genius.
- The Soloist.
- The Expert.

I identify with the perfectionist because I set very high goals for myself and feel like I do not measure up when I fail to achieve them. I sometimes lean towards the soloist because I tend to believe that I have to do things myself if I want them done right.

Therefore, my courage formula begins with overcoming my perfectionist tendencies. I was forced to learn to accept my mistakes as a part of my journey and celebrate my accomplishments, no matter how small. I now understand that I cannot allow my fear of producing an imperfect product or service to prevent me from moving forward.

That is just the beginning of my courage formula. My background in math compelled me to create a formula to describe the process of developing courage. Here it is:

C2- Clarity and Commitment

I created a vision, wrote it down and created a visual representation of it in the form of a vision board. I have to look at that vision board daily to get clarity about what I want for the future. This reminder helps me organize my priorities for the day that will help make the ultimate vision a reality.

In essence, I use my vision board to gain clarity on the small tasks I need to complete daily to achieve success. Clarity then helps me develop the commitment I need to step into the spotlight despite my fears. Both features work in tandem to further help me overcome my perfectionist tendencies and develop the courage necessary to overcome my fears.

A- Accountability

Courage often becomes prevalent when there is no choice but to be courageous. An accountability partner has helped me commit to situations where courage really is my only choice.

My accountability partner is my best friend, Shonda. We have an agreement where she and I work together to set reasonable weekly goals, not the lofty goals I would create because I am a perfectionist.

She checks in with me at the end of the week to get an update on my progress. If I have not accomplished what I set out to do, I pay her $100. I jolly well know that I cannot afford to lose $100 and keep funding Shonda's weekly trips to the salon, so that gives me the motivation I need to stop allowing fear to hold me back.

S- Strengthen the Network

I have said this several times throughout this book; it's such an important point that I had to say it again. I am growing my network of like-minded black sisters who are not afraid to dream big and support each other.

The support of such networks helps me develop confidence. It also helps me get the mentorship I need to test the opportunities that come my way so that I can determine whether they are the right fit.

I also benefit from honest feedback and constructive criticism. Both are necessary to improve my decision-making process. They also help me see the blind spots I missed because I was too close to the process.

How can you get the courage you need?

Step 1: Determine whether you are suffering from Imposter Syndrome.

I encourage you to read Dr. Young's book to determine whether you are suffering from Imposter Syndrome and how you can thrive in spite of it. My main issue is perfectionism but yours may be one of the other five listed. The best way to find out is to read the book and learn from it.

Step 2: Apply the Courage Formula.

Get the clarity you need daily to take the small steps necessary for accomplishing your vision. Use that clarity to fuel your commitment to getting things done, despite your fear.

One of the easiest ways to step into your fears is to take tiny steps. Do not think about running the whole marathon, think about running the first 100 meters.

As long as you keep moving forward, your belief and courage will be strengthened.

Find an accountability partner you can trust. Work with that person to attach appropriate consequences for not accomplishing your goals. You will want to avoid the consequence. This avoidance increases your chances of killing fear and getting things done.

Keep strengthening your network of sisters. Your network can never be too strong. Keep searching for black women groups you can join. Keep attending networking events. Keep meeting new people so that you can be a part of a supportive community that gives you the courage to keep going.

Lastly, have you considered doing challenges? Experts have shown that challenges are an effective way to harness courage and get you into the habit of doing.

So, you have been meaning to launch your YouTube Channel. How about doing a "30-days to launch my channel" challenge? Having something you can commit to, with a looming deadline, can help you let go of fear and embrace each day courageously.

Use your courage to take the first step.

My public speaking story demonstrates that you really only need the courage to take the first step. It is never an easy first step to take. However, it is one that can change your life for the better.

Here are some questions that you should ask as you prepare to build your courage and take the first step.

What is the worst that can happen?

My great grandmother Mavis would always ask me this question while I was growing up, "What is the worst that could happen?" She is one of the most courageous persons I have ever met.

She came to America from Jamaica in her 30s without a single dollar to her name and managed to walk with courage and use her power to pull herself out of poverty. She often told me that it is easy to be courageous if you can identify the worst possible outcome.

Let us look at an example of how her philosophy works.

You notice a job on a job board website that is right up your alley. But you are hesitant about applying. Your mind is playing tricks on you, telling you that you may not be the right fit or that no one will actually read your resume.

These thoughts demonstrate a lack of courage.

What if you asked yourself, "What is the worst that could happen if I applied for this job?".

The worst that can happen is you not getting the job offer. Does this reality harm you in any way? Sure, you'll be disappointed, but you'll eventually move on to bigger and better opportunities.

Your courage will be strengthened the quicker you

realize the worst possible outcomes will not harm you. It is better to have tried rather than live with the regret of not trying at all.

Is my fear serving or hurting me?

Fear is necessary. In some cases, it prevents us from getting into dangerous situations. For instance, the fear of getting burnt would prevent you from touching a lit burner on a gas stove.

It is important for you to distinguish between fear that serves you and fear that hurts you. Fear that serves you is that necessary fear that keeps you out of dangerous situations. On the other hand, fear that hurts you is irrational and often an excuse we use to prevent us from taking risks.

You can use the strategies I described in Chapter Four to overcome your irrational fear. Couple that with the strategies presented in this chapter for building courage and you will be on your way towards your next big step.

What is the recurring fear I have that I need the courage to overcome?

You may have some fears that just keep coming back. Identify them and apply the courage formula so that you can overcome them.

They may return occasionally. However, you will learn how to push them aside the more your courage grows.

Our role models have also worked hard at pushing

through their fears and, with each tiny step they made, they grew stronger and stronger. Be like the lioness. Be brave. Be courageous.

REFLECTION QUESTIONS

1. What struggles have you been facing with developing courage?
2. What is the important first step you need to take to get to the next level?
3. Who is going to be your accountability partner?
4. What is the worst that can happen?

CHAPTER 9

There's Power in Your Presence

> "When I dare to be powerful, to use my strength in the service of my vision, then it becomes less and less important whether I am afraid."
>
> ~Audre Lorde

I WAS QUIVERING IN my boots as I approached the ornate boardroom doors. This was the first time I had ever been to a board meeting at our corporate office. I had spent several weeks preparing for this day but still could not shake the anxiety lurking over my shoulder.

My fear did not really come from a lack of confidence in my knowledge and the work I had done. Instead, it came from my fear of being a black woman in a room filled with white men. It is a fear that made me second-guess every move I made, every word I spoke.

The fear seemed justified a few minutes later when the Chief Finance Officer (CFO) looked at me and said,

"Why should I listen to you? Your kind doesn't understand what goes on in the big leagues."

I literally had to bite my tongue to prevent myself from saying something that would mar my reputation. Eventually, the CFO gave me the respect I deserved because I ***proved*** why everyone in that room should listen to me, but I left that board meeting with my blood boiling.

Here I was, forgetting the ***power*** I have as a strong, black woman. I was no longer the black math teacher from Florida with facial atrophy on the left-side of her face. Instead, I was a woman who had worked hard to rise up the ranks and become a respected leader in this finance company despite being surrounded by primarily white colleagues.

It was then that I remembered the words from an article I had read recently. It was written by Ariane Hunter and entitled *What Women of Color Need to Know About Building a Personal Brand.* The most powerful message I got from that article was the need to "use [my] cultural roots as an asset to build influence and open doors to projects and media channels that regularly look for people with [my] background."

The only way to step into the power of my presence and stop second-guessing myself was for me to step into an organization where who I am as a black woman was understood and valued. I should not be in a place where I feel anxious about entering a room because of the color of my skin.

It was not time for me to start the Melona Financial Group. I still needed to gain more experience and industry knowledge. Additionally, I still needed to expand my network.

But I made a decision that day after I walked out of that boardroom. I had to find a senior-level position at a company where my cultural roots and background are viewed as assets.

Easier said than done.

I had already spent about three years building roots at this company. It would be difficult for me to find a comparable job in another company without probably working again from the bottom up.

Finding these companies was also a challenge. There were not many financial companies in my region at the time that genuinely appreciated cultural diversity in the workplace and gave black women the respect and opportunities they deserved.

LinkedIn provided a golden ticket.

Little did I know I would find my golden ticket on LinkedIn. I made a deliberate attempt to rebrand my LinkedIn profile so that I would attract the positions I was seeking. Additionally, I networked with other LinkedIn users to open myself up to more opportunities.

Here is what my process looked like.

1. Create a tagline that summarizes the unique skills I have and services I offer.

2. Craft a narrative in my About section that tells my story and does not sound like a robotic, dry Cover Letter.
3. Add valuable content to the Featured section of my profile.
4. Get strong recommendations from people I have worked with.
5. Explain how I delivered results in each of my roles for the Skills and Experience section.
6. Write at least two LinkedIn articles per month expressing my views about the current state of the finance industry.
7. Reach out to decision-makers in organizations I wanted to work with.

My strategy greatly increased my visibility and I was pleased to receive a message from a CEO of an investment firm for black professionals. He was even offering me a salary increase.

This experience taught me the power of establishing a strong online presence. How I portrayed myself online needed to be a true reflection of my personal brand and my vision.

I created a website and became very deliberate about what I posted on all my social media channels. This is not the book for explaining how to create a website but I will say that I have been able to increase my visibility through creating a responsive, attractive website with fast page load speeds and an active blog.

People in my network are also clearer about what I

stand for and the power I represent as a self-assured black woman in finance.

There is power in my online presence.

Why should you dare to be powerful?

You are possibly in a situation at work or community where you feel like you cannot stand in your power and greatness as a black woman. Unfortunately, it is a sad reality we face as black women in America.

There is nothing wrong with demonstrating your power online in a way that is respectful and inclusive. Here are four things I suggest you do online so that you can open doors to projects and media channels searching for people just like you.

Create a strong LinkedIn profile.

LinkedIn has developed a solid reputation as ***the*** platform for professionals to network. However, too many LinkedIn profiles are boring and lack the pizzaz necessary to help readers understand who this person is beyond what is on a Curriculum Vitae (CV).

Here are some tips to help you create the right LinkedIn profile.

1. Choose a professionally shot profile picture that captures you smiling against a solid background. People respond better to pictures where the person is smiling.
2. Create a professional personal brand statement.

This statement differs from the one you created in chapter five. It is something short that portrays what you do in your own unique way. Therefore, it goes far beyond your job title.

Example: I help businesses increase their ROI by 105% on average through proper financial forecasting and investment analysis.

This personal brand statement becomes your LinkedIn tagline and provides the framework you will use to develop the rest of your profile and produce content across all the platforms you use.

1. Write a captivating About section. This section is your opportunity to help the reader understand your story and how it aligns with your personal brand. My About section includes the fact that I am particularly passionate about the black community.
2. Include your videos and website links in your Featured section that support the narrative you have created.
3. Clearly describe the results you have helped the organizations you have worked for achieve in the Work History section.
4. Post a LinkedIn article at least once per month that shares your unique perspectives and shows that you know what you are talking about.

Pay attention to other social media networks, too.

You may not be looking for business-to-business (B2B) or corporate opportunities, which is okay. There are other social media platforms you can use to strengthen your online presence.

Think about the social media platforms your target audience frequently uses. Those are the social media platforms you should also use if you want to increase your chances of reaching them.

This is not a guide for creating a strong social media profile. However, I can give you some general tips to help you build a following that is authentically interested in what you have to say.

1. Be authentic. Do not use social media as a way to show people what you ***think*** they want to see. Your audience wants to learn more about you—what you stand for, your interests and your perspectives beyond the workplace. Show them that.
2. Post at least twice per day. Your posts do not have to be elaborate but consistently posting is important for building intrigue and keeping your audience engaged. Posts could be as simple as a motivational quote or as elaborate as a live video chat. Use a content calendar to help you keep on track.
3. Read and respond to comments and direct messages (DMs). DMs can be a treasure chest

for opportunities you never thought possible. Instagram, for instance, does not notify users when a message request is sent so you should check your messages daily to avoid missing these message requests.

Create a website.

We often think that websites are reserved for people who have businesses or own blogs. However, websites are such versatile online platforms for showcasing your personal brand.

Use a website that has your name and a custom domain such as .com or .net. When people type your name into a search bar, one of the first things that will come up is your website if you structure it this way.

But what should you put on your website? Here are some suggestions:

1. Attractive photos that show you as a professional and/or a family woman.
2. A video (or two) that explains your journey.
3. Blog posts, similar to those you post on LinkedIn, that help establish you as a thought-leader.
4. If you are feeling inspired, you could probably even host an online course on your website!

YouTube videos can also grab attention.

You may not be much of a writer, but you may be a great conversationalist. Why not create a YouTube video series? Your aim is not necessarily to build a huge following. Instead, you are trying to help people learn more about you and your thoughts on what is happening in your industry.

These videos also increase your online visibility. So, they are a great addition if you want to build a powerful online presence.

The extent of your power extends beyond the virtual world.

Throughout this book, I have stressed the importance of joining organizations that support the black community. That is where you will find mentors and like-minded people who can help you be bold enough to own your power.

However, it is not about joining these organizations to take as much as you can without giving anything in return. You should genuinely care about the causes they advocate for and ***do something about them.***

Be an active member. This is one of the many ways you can use your strength in service of your vision. Attend the meetings and rallies. Mentor young black teens. Do what you can to make a difference in your community beyond your computer screen.

Remember to take care of you.

Social media and community activism are time-consuming activities. If you are not careful, they will consume so much of your time that you start letting yourself go.

Do not let that happen, girl! You still deserve to pamper yourself and be happy. You cannot pour from an empty cup.

I keep my cup full by:

1. Knowing when to say, "No!".
2. Setting a daily priority list where I do the tasks that require most focus during my peak hours and leave less involved tasks (such as checking emails) for times when I am not usually at my peak. This minimizes my stress levels.
3. Taking at least an hour daily to do something I love.
4. Planning a trip with my friends to another state at least twice per year. I look forward to these trips!
5. Treating myself to a spa day about once per month. If I'm being honest, this ends up being once every two months sometimes.

The ball is in your court.

No one can portray the power of your presence except you. There is no one else in this world who does things just like you. You have so much to offer this world and the only way the world will truly appreciate your value is if you own your power.

Remember, however, that you cannot pour from an

empty cup. It is not necessarily about striking a balance because that really is an elusive concept for women like us who have ***so much to do***. But you cannot just let yourself go.

Make time to enjoy life! You do not need to be superwoman 24/7. It is okay to make time for you.

Step past fear and use the strength of your online presence and the organizations in which you are involved to leave an indelible mark on this world. The ball is in your court. What will they write on your epitaph?

REFLECTION QUESTIONS

1. What changes do you need to make to your LinkedIn profile?
2. How can you restructure your time so that you are able to write at least one thought-provoking article per month?
3. What YouTube series can you start?
4. How can you make a difference in the lives of people within your immediate community?

PART 4

Walk into Your Destiny

"Your life is your story and
the journey ahead of you is
the journey to fulfill your own
purpose and potential."
~Kerry Washington

CHAPTER 10

Find the Right King for your Kingdom

> "The 'love' in the love story is how you come through trials. The passion, the lust—that's easy. The love story is how you come out in love after hardship."
>
> -Pauletta Washington

I HAVE BEEN THROUGH the ringer a few times when it comes to dating and relationships. There was the colorful Jamal who ironically turned out to be a racist misogynist. The guy of my dreams became a bunch of hallucinations after he died in a car accident.

There were other guys in between who I never really quite clicked with for one reason or another.

So much drama!

My dating life was filled with more lows than highs. Until I met Denzel.

It was the middle of September and I was busy with a

slew of meetings preparing for the final (and busiest) quarter of the year.

I was hurriedly walking towards my next meeting a few blocks away, my stilettos clicking against the pavement.

As usual, I was absorbed in my phone—responding to messages, checking emails and looking at my to-do list. I really was not paying attention to where I was going.

So, it was not surprising when I collided with this tall, charming black man dressed in a crisp royal blue suit. My bag fell on the ground and the papers it contained scattered along the pavement.

"I am so sorry!" I exclaimed in embarrassment as I knelt down to gather the papers.

He smiled as he helped me gather the papers and said, "That's okay. You should really look where you're going, though."

I laughed nervously, stood up and started looking for my phone so that I could resume my journey.

"Are you looking for this?" he asked while holding my phone with a smirk on his face as he looked intently into my eyes.

There was something about the way he looked at me, like he could see into the depths of who I am. It made me a bit uncomfortable and I just wanted to get out of there as quickly as I could.

"Uh, yeah. Thanks."

"Can I get your number so that I can call you sometime?"

"Uh...I don't know about that. I'm super busy and actually running late for a meeting…"

He took my hand and wrote his number on my palm.

"Call me when you get some time," he said.

I honestly was not ready to jump back into the dating scene and figured I would just forget that encounter ever happened.

What happened next actually surprised me.

We were taking a lunch break from a board meeting and I was in the lunchroom ready to pour some coffee. A handsome stranger's hand brushed against mine as I reached for the coffee canister.

My heart skipped a beat when I looked up and realized it was the same guy from earlier this morning.

"Are you stalking me now?" I asked.

"Well, I actually work here and needed some coffee as an energy boost," he replied as he sat in one of the chairs in the room and looked at me in amusement.

We chatted for the next 30 minutes and I was amazed by how well we connected. I was so intrigued by the fact that I caved and gave him my number.

Things progressed quickly and we officially became a couple about two months later, much sooner than I expected. This relationship has not been perfect, but I strongly believe he is the right king for my kingdom.

All my relationships have taught me a lot about love, pain, betrayal and knowing when to let go. Denzel has taught me why, despite everything I have been through, that it is important to have a supportive partner.

Sure, we are strong, independent women and we do not ***need*** a man, but that does not mean, however, that the right partner will not add value to our lives. That is why I am sharing the lessons I have learned about relationships over the past few years and why Denzel has been the right match for me.

Four lessons I have learnt from my relationships:

1. Pay attention to red flags.

Any relationship expert (or even your closest friends) will tell you to pay attention to the red flags in your relationship. You and I know that doing this is easier said than done, especially when you have fallen in love.

We tend to make the mistake of thinking we can change a person. It is clear as day that he has undesirable traits that you cannot change about him, yet you are still holding on to the hope that things will get better one day.

I mentioned my ex-boyfriend, Jamal, in Chapter Four, the racist misogynist. Overhearing the conversation he had with his friend was the final straw for me, but that relationship should have ended months before, if I'm being truly honest.

There were red flags a mile long, but I chose to ignore

them because Jamal was the picture-perfect image of the guy I ***should*** be with. He was a colorful character, smart, had a great job and came from a good home.

However, his attitude stunk worse than a skunk. He would say mean things to me occasionally and I did not realize that I was actually being mentally abused until years after we had broken up. I honestly thought that I could teach him to be more sensitive and compassionate—that I could change him for the better.

That would ***never*** happen. Jamal is who he is and there was nothing I could do or say to change him. Thankfully, I overheard his conversation and ended the relationship before I fell into the trap of marrying him for all the wrong reasons.

2. Be open to explore.

There is no perfect guy who will check off all the boxes on your list. Whether we want to admit it or not, we all have a list; some of us go to the extreme of never giving a man the time of day if he is missing one of those ideal traits.

Denzel does not fit into the mold of my ideal man. He is not earning a six-figure salary and is actually seven years younger than me. Nevertheless, he is perfect for me because we connect on so many levels—intellectually, spiritually, emotionally—the list goes on. He is also highly ambitious and I know that we can become a power couple as we support each other's dreams.

I would not have given Denzel a second glance back in

the day. However, I am glad I have changed and opened myself up to experience a beautiful relationship.

3. A relationship is about helping each other become your best selves.

I have learnt that I cannot enter a relationship expecting the other person to make me happy and meet all my complex needs. Instead, a relationship is a partnership where two independent people come ***together*** to help each other improve.

Denzel and I know how to be happy independently and live full lives. However, we know that we have to support each other and help each other grow. We are not leeches who suck each other dry.

4. Things take time.

Patience is not a virtue I possess. In the past, I have expected my boyfriends to have things all figured out and be ready to support a family from the get-go. That is not the way things work in the real world.

I think mainstream media has a significant role to play in how we perceive relationships. It is actually quite rare to find a man who has all his shit together. Therefore, you have to decide what shit you are willing to work with and how much time you are going to give him to step up to where he needs to be.

Be realistic. For instance, I cannot expect Denzel to start earning a six-figure salary in three months. Stepping up to that level will require him to either form his own company or improve his qualifications. He has chosen the latter and that will take time.

On the flip side, empty promises are meaningless. If your man works as a dishwasher but has aspirations to become a world class chef, he should be taking the necessary steps to make that happen. If he is just sitting on his rump not doing anything, he is probably not the man for you.

Sure, things take time, but progress will take an eternity to manifest if steps are not being taken to make it happen.

What makes a man the right partner?

Denzel entered my life in a way I did not expect. I was doing fine on my own, crushing my goals and moving closer towards my dream of starting Melona Financial Group. I also know how to be happy in my own skin and enjoy my own company, so it is not like I felt terrible loneliness I thought someone else could fill.

Instead, Denzel has demonstrated that he is the right partner for me because he:

1. Balances me out. For instance, I can often become overly worried about the future, but he knows how to calm me down and help me focus on what I need to do in the present. I did not realize how much I needed this balance until recently.

2. Is not egotistic. He understands that we are equal partners and knows that we are there to support each other. The relationship is not all about him and it is not all about me.
3. Gives me the respect I deserve. I never feel belittled in his presence. The respect he shows me boosts my confidence even further and gives me the push I need to make things happen.
4. Helps me see that I can have a life outside of work. Sure, I know I can hang out with my friends, but they have their own lives and families to take care of. In fact, I was the only person in my circle who was single. Denzel has shown me the importance of having my own life outside of work and friends.

Three tips to help you find the right man for you:

1. Love who you are before trying to love someone else.

Oftentimes, we enter relationships hoping the other person can fix us. We feel unworthy and harbor self-deprecating thoughts we hope a knight in shining can fix. That is not fair to our partners and will only lead to long-term problems in the relationship.

Therefore, you have to take the time to get over the negative thoughts and experiences preventing you from loving and appreciating yourself. Learn how to have fun being single and enjoy your own company. That way, you can enter a relationship as a complete individual rather than someone who is looking for a partner to fill the missing pieces.

The amazing thing about it, too, is that shifting your focus in this way will help you attract the type of man you seek. It is like you become a magnet for the men who will add value to your life rather than waste your time.

2. Be open to unexpected possibilities.

Throw your darn list into the trash. No man will fit into a perfect mold. Of course, it is important to have standards, but you will not find the right man for you if you set the bar too high. Be open to unexpected possibilities.

I would never have thought I would enter a relationship with someone as young as Denzel. However, I know at least three couples where the woman is older than the man and they have been happily married for several years. In fact, I know a couple where the man is ***10 years*** younger than the woman and they have been happily married for more than 30 years.

That fact made me appreciate that age is just a number and what matters more is the character of the person and how you work together as a unit. It is more about how this man thinks and behaves than it is about his age and wealth.

Now, don't get me wrong. I am not saying you should start a relationship with a younger man. I am just sharing my experience and using it as an example for being open to unexpected possibilities.

3. Stop ignoring red flags.

Some of the red flags you should look for include:

- Overly jealous.
- Manipulative.
- Irresponsible, immature and unpredictable.
- A secretive past.
- No closure from past relationships.
- Him making you feel insecure.

I am sure there are many others, but these are the red flags I have encountered in my relationships. Do not ignore any red flags that may pop up as your relationship progresses.

REFLECTION QUESTIONS

1. What mistakes have you made in your past relationships?
2. Are you in a relationship now where you have been ignoring red flags?
3. What do you need to do to be more comfortable in your own skin?
4. Are you afraid to fall in love? If so, why?

CHAPTER 11

Consistency Brings Results

> "Consistency breathes life into your dreams."
>
> ~Erika Rae Bailey

I want you to glow brightly in your marvelous light. However, I know glowing may be difficult because it requires consistency. There will be challenges, stress, disappointment and failure. The effort required to consistently push through all of that can often be too great to bear.

The reality of this struck me while I was staring at my vision board one Sunday evening. An overwhelming feeling of exhaustion overcame me.

I began to question why I had even decided to embark on this journey. There were so many sleepless nights, doors being slammed in my face, and emotional struggle as I grappled with the loss of my first love; so many things were threatening my resolve to move forward.

But I still kept pushing.

My *why* was bigger than the problems and struggles I had endured. The exhaustion I felt was only a sign that I needed rest, not that I needed to give up.

I still needed to consistently show up and do what was necessary to make that vision board a reality.

How I Built a Habit of Consistency

Let me be completely honest with you. Consistency is one of the things I have struggled with the most on my glow journey.

I know how to put in the work to make things happen. However, my willpower to keep pushing when things are not going exactly the way I had hoped sometimes wanes.

Dealing with this struggle forced me to learn how to develop a habit of consistency. Here are the nuggets of wisdom I have learned throughout this journey.

Pay attention to the small steps.

This may seem obvious to you, but it was not something I realized until much later in life. If you are consistent in the small things, the bigger things become easier.

Here is a good example. I had to abruptly adjust to my boyfriend moving into my cramped apartment. There was not enough space to begin with for me to work comfortably. Add him to the mix and *everything* at home suddenly became a distraction.

My apartment is small, so the living room essentially functions as my TV room, office, dining room and chill spot. So, when I try to work and he wants to watch TV, the TV becomes a problem.

I had to make some small changes. I moved the TV into the bedroom and set up my office space in a nook where my back was turned away from all distractions.

I also started getting up at 5:00 am (not waking up and then rolling over in bed). Doing this consistently ***every*** morning meant that I was able to accomplish more than I did before. Being consistent with the ***small things*** helped me keep up with the bigger tasks that demanded my attention.

Daily prioritizing matters.

It is never my intention to wake up and commit to ***not*** getting things done throughout the day. There are some days, however, where I become so flustered by everything I have to do that I either end up doing nothing at all or focus on the wrong tasks.

Over the past year, I have realized that I need a daily prioritization strategy. So, I created this task scale that I use to rank each of the tasks I need to complete that day.

Time

How much time does this task approximately require?

1 - 15 minutes

2 - 30 minutes

3 - 60 minutes

4 - 90 minutes

Effort

What is the difficulty level of this task? Does it require a lot of effort?

1 - Easy-Peasy

2 - Gotta Give a Little Push

3 - This One is a Doozy

4 - All Systems Go!

I end each evening by preparing my task list for the next day. Here is how my process works.

1. Write each task down. The order does not matter at this point.
2. Use the rating scale to rate each task based on time and effort.
3. Rearrange the list so that the tasks that require the most time and effort are scheduled during my peak hours.

Let me illustrate this using a hypothetical scenario. It

is Sunday evening and I am preparing my task list for Monday.

Step 1: Write each task down.

- Complete Weekly report for Previous Week.
- Create an Investment Policy Statement (IPS) for Client X.
- Meet with the owner of Company X at 10:00 am.
- Review Personal Investments.

Step 2: Use the rating scale. (T represents Time and E represents Effort)

- Complete Weekly report for Previous Week - T (1) E(2).
- Create an Investment Policy Statement (IPS) for Client X - T(4) E(4).
- Meet with the owner of Company X at 10:00 am - T(3) E(3).
- Review Personal Investments - T(1) E(1).

Step 3: Rearrange tasks and create a complete schedule for the day.

Note that one of the tasks already had a set time so I would not have had any flexibility to move it elsewhere.

My peak hours (the hours when I am most productive)

are 8:00 am to midday. Therefore, I need to schedule the most difficult tasks for that time.

5:00 am to 5:30 am - Meditate and prepare my mind for the day.

5:30 am to 6:00am - Exercise

6:00 am to 7:00 am - Eat and Bathe

7:00 am to 8:00 am - Catch up on emails and social media. *

8:00 am to 9: 30 am- Create an IPS for Client X **

9:30 am to 9:45 am - BREAK ***

9:45 am to 9:55 am - Quick preparation for meeting with Company X

10:00 am to 11:00 am - Meeting with Company X

11:00 am to 11:15 am - Review meeting notes and highlight tasks I need to complete.

11:15 am to 11:30 am - BREAK

11:30 am to 11: 45 am - Complete weekly report for previous week.

11:45 am to 12:45 pm - BREAK

12:45 pm to 1:00 pm - Review personal investments.

I would now have the rest of the day to fit in other tasks that may have popped up unexpectedly.

*Emails and social media are another huge distraction for me. Therefore, I actually schedule them into my day.

** Remember that my peak hours are from 8:00 am to midday. Therefore, I put the task that required the most time and effort at the earliest possible time in the day. If I do not complete it within that timeframe, I can always go back to it in the time I have available after 1:00 pm.

***Breaks are important for your sanity and health! It is important to take your eyes off the computer screen throughout the day and give your skeleton a break by walking around at various intervals.

Small accomplishments deserve rewards.

We often think that rewards have to be big in order to be satisfying. Additionally, we tend to limit rewards to huge accomplishments.

That approach is a lie! Small rewards for small accomplishments give us the motivation to keep pushing forward.

I like to reward myself with breaks because my life is so hectic that breaks often seem like an elusive concept. Other small rewards I may give to myself include blending up my favorite smoothie or buying the ingredients for a new cookie recipe.

The trick with rewards, though, is that they should be pegged to a task. It is an "if…then" type of scenario. If I complete this task, then I will reward myself with X. I cannot get that reward unless I complete the task. Sticking to this requires discipline, but I have found it to be a strategy that works.

How can you maintain consistency?

What works for one person may not work for the next. I appreciate this fact and will not necessarily say that what I have done to improve my consistency will work for you. Nevertheless, here are my suggestions for some of the things that you can try.

Make small changes to your daily routine.

You would be surprised by how even the smallest change can make a huge difference. The trick is identifying where a small change needs to be made so that you can make the right adjustments. These tips could help you really pinpoint where the small change is needed.

1. Identify what is preventing you from maintaining consistency. Are you easily distracted? Have you taken on too many responsibilities?
2. Break down everything you need to do daily into the smallest possible task. Is there something that you can change about this small task to increase the chances of you completing the bigger task?
3. Identify small habits that may be missing from

your routine. I was missing the small task of unplugging my TV and turning away from all distractions in my cramped apartment. Is there a small habit that you need to add to your daily routine to make a big impact?

Use a time-blocking strategy.

Your challenge may be understanding how to prioritize the tasks you need to complete each day. If you do not prioritize your tasks, you may end up completing less important tasks first and never really getting around to the most important tasks.

I described my time-blocking strategy earlier where I prioritize my daily tasks based on time and effort. That strategy may not work for you, but that does not mean there is not another that will work perfectly.

Do your research to find a time-blocking strategy that works for you so that you can give your daily tasks the priority they deserve. I guarantee that it will make a difference.

Never forget to take a break.

Burnout is a very real problem. It can threaten all progress you have made towards your goals. Girl, you really do not want to start from scratch! So, avoiding burnout is paramount.

Hard work and discipline are important. In fact, that

is all we know as black women. We just press the "Go" button and ***work, work, work and work*** some more.

Living like that neither benefits you nor the people you serve. Sure, I know you feel guilty about taking a break or doing something you enjoy because you just have so much to do. But ***girl***, living like that just ain't gonna work because burnout will soon come knocking at your door.

I appreciate that there will be sleepless nights because I have been there and done that. However, there ***must*** be some downtime and you ***must*** take breaks in between all the work you need to do. Recharging your batteries helps you keep spinning the wheels of consistency.

Take your accountability partner seriously.

I discussed the importance of having an accountability partner in Chapter Eight as an important way to develop courage and stick to your goals. The same is true if you want to remain consistent.

Your accountability partner could be your personal trainer, your partner, your friend, online/local communities or even your kids. You can even hire accountability partners! A quick search on Google will provide you with many marketplaces that have specialist accountability partners for a range of activities.

As an example, if you are looking for an accountability partner to help keep you on track with writing your business plan, you would find an accountability partner that specializes in business development.

Studies have shown that once you tell someone other than yourself about your goals and the action steps you need to take, you are more committed to doing the work and staying consistent. You will not want to explain why you did not do what you said you would do.

Reward yourself for small accomplishments.

Stop holding on to this feeling of guilt for loving yourself, taking care of yourself and paying attention to your needs while also looking out for everyone else. There is nothing wrong with rewarding yourself for taking small steps towards your goals.

With that said, it is still important for you to make wise financial decisions. I am not saying that you should reward yourself with a $1000 pair of red-bottom heels because you got up and exercised this morning. That would be foolish.

Small rewards can be treating yourself to a healthy (but delicious) snack, watching a few Netflix episodes with your partner or having a game night with your little kings and queens. You really do not need to do anything extravagant to reward yourself for small accomplishments. Just remember to reward yourself.

Consistency is hard but it is worthwhile.

Consistency may become one of your biggest struggles as you continue this journey of glowing in your beautiful Nubian empress light. However, you will reap huge rewards if you get it right.

There is really no secret formula to maintaining consistency. It is really about trial and error to find a strategy that truly works for you. I have mentioned some strategies in this chapter to improve your consistency, but you can also experiment with other strategies and ideas to see what is best suited to you. Just remember that you will get results if you are consistently taking the right steps.

REFLECTION QUESTIONS

1. What issues are you having with your consistency? How can you address those issues?
2. What small changes do you need to make to your routine?
3. Who do you know that would make a great accountability partner?
4. How can you make taking care of yourself a priority?

CHAPTER 12

Keep Those Blinkers On

> "I don't focus on what I'm up against. I focus on my goals and try to ignore the rest."
>
> -Venus Williams

EMBRACE YOUR ECLECTIC beauty as a strong, black woman. You are ***not*** inferior. Instead, you are a rare gem with the ability to transform anything into a masterpiece.

The reality is that we are fighting a war against deeply ingrained thoughts and beliefs about racial and gender discrimination that have been passed on for centuries. Together, we can change this reality through the work we do in the organizations we serve or through the enterprises that we build.

We should never stop fighting. Instead, we must continue fighting hard to prove our worth and claim what is rightfully ours. It is messed up and it would be great if we lived in a world where skin color and gender were not used to belittle what we do.

Nevertheless, what ultimately matters is how you view yourself and the contribution you can make to this world. As Venus Williams rightly said, your mind should be focused on pressing forward with your goals rather than the odds stacked against you. That is how you will walk into your destiny.

There are four powerful facts that you should remember.

Your thoughts and feelings are important.

It is exhausting to continuously portray an image of a strong, black woman who is not afraid to stand up for what she believes is right. I ***know*** that living this reality takes a mental toll and can lead to high levels of depression and anxiety.

Therefore, you need to be in-tune with your thoughts and feelings. I am not saying that you need to turn up the speakers and tell the world exactly how you are feeling and thinking. All I am saying is that you need to pay attention to your mental health.

Do not fall into the trap of pushing your thoughts and feelings aside because you need to be strong for everyone else and you do not want to appear weak. I have been there, done that and almost had a mental breakdown because of it.

Find a trusted friend or counselor who can help you get those thoughts off your chest. If you choose to fight your mental battles alone, your journey towards your destiny will become even more difficult. Instead, make a conscious effort to address your thoughts and feelings so that you can have more mental space to make your dreams a reality.

Let your voice *be heard.*

There are times when your thoughts need to be vocalized to a larger audience. Our ancestors were silenced because they were viewed as dirty, worthless slaves. How dare a black slave speak out against her master? That backward way of thinking cannot thrive in the 21st century.

Speak your truth even if it makes others uncomfortable. But speak that truth with respect and dignity. Support your statements with facts and let those who need to know understand that your voice makes a difference. Speak because you stand for integrity, justice and the rights you have as a black woman living in America.

Your creativity *makes a difference.*

We have spoken about fear a lot in this book. I fervently believe that everyone experiences fear about taking a big step towards their goals. For some, that fear drives them. For others, that fear forces them to hide in their comfort zones.

But you see when you give into that fear, you stifle your creativity. You create the best environment for creativity to thrive when you push the boundaries a bit, think outside the box and step outside of your comfort zone.

Tap into your creativity as you walk into your destiny. Unexpected (and even expected) things will happen as you make your voice heard. Some of these things, such as losing your job, will throw you for a loop. How you use your creativity to get out of that funk and maintain your momentum towards your dream is all that ultimately matters.

Your unique traits *are valuable.*

You were not created to contribute to the wealth of the graveyard. There should be no reason for you to apologize for being authentically you. Who ***you*** are is a gift to the world and anyone who is telling you otherwise does not deserve a space in your life.

Focus on living life the best way you know how. Life is not about comparing yourself with others and wondering why you cannot be like everyone else. It is about fitting into your unique place in this world using everything that makes you unique.

Understand and appreciate this reality. Although your gender and race define you, they are not what make you truly unique. Who you are at your core and how you choose to make a contribution to this world, no matter how messed up it is, makes a huge difference.

What happens when life gets in the way?

Life will never be perfect. You have used most of this book to plan and prepare for a brighter future, but things will not always happen exactly as planned.

I have a friend who was on her way towards becoming a sought-after executive in the ed-tech industry. She was completing her master's degree and was also next in line for a promotion. Her heart dropped when she discovered that she was pregnant.

Her relationship was on the rocks so it looked like she would be raising this child herself. One night, she poured her heart out to me through streams of tears as she pondered what her next move would be.

I told her to **keep those blinkers on**. Sure, having a baby would set her back a bit, especially since she was placed on bed rest in her sixth month of pregnancy, for health reasons. But that did not mean her dream would die.

She took a leave of absence from school so that she could take the bed rest and spend time with her new-born baby when she arrived. Additionally, she leaned heavily on her support system of friends and family to help her with babysitting when she had to work.

Guess what? She is now the Chief Technical Officer of an ed-tech firm with over 500,000 clients nationwide. She also successfully completed her degree. Although her dream did not exactly follow her timeline, she was still able to make that dream a reality.

I have shared this story because I want you to understand that life getting in the way should not force you to give up on your dreams. The trick is to determine the adjustments you need to make for each curveball life throws at you.

Let me tell you this, curveballs will come your way. But you are stronger than you think. So, breathe in, be courageous and keep moving towards your goals.

Do not let black stereotypes hold you back.

Black female athletes often experience their fair share of stereotypes. Debi Thomas, the first black woman to take home a figure skating Olympics medal for the U.S., is a classic example. She often faced criticism from judges and the media for coming across as aggressive and overly competitive—the stereotypical representation of a black American woman.

She could have used that criticism as an excuse to end her career. Instead, she famously said, "A lot of people think they want to do something, but when the going gets tough, they just don't have the will to stick with it." She ignored the naysayers and became a figure skating legend.

Simone Manuel is another example of a black female athlete who chose to ignore racial stereotypes as she pursued her career. There was great fanfare when she became the first black American to win an Olympic gold medal in the 100m freestyle. She said in a New York Times interview, "I would like there to be a day when there are more of us and it's not Simone, the black swimmer, because the title black swimmer makes it seem like I'm not supposed to be able to win a gold medal or I'm not supposed to be able to break records."

Preach it, girl! I long for the day when we move away from congratulating black women for their accomplishments as if we are not supposed to achieve these feats. In fact, I want you to look beyond your skin color and gender and just keep pushing towards that gold medal of success.

Use every setback as a comeback.

Taraji Henson's story demonstrates the power of moving beyond a setback. She always wanted to be an actress, but she was rejected from Duke Ellington School of the Arts in Washington. Her family encouraged her to keep pushing so she moved to Los Angeles with her son and landed a role in a small film.

She still could have chosen to call it quits because she did not get another acting gig immediately afterwards. I am sure she probably questioned whether pursuing her dream was truly worth it, especially when she had to provide for her child as a single mother.

Nevertheless, she kept pushing forward and landed another film role three years later that catapulted her career. Despite everything around her telling her to quit, she kept those blinkers on and continued to move forward.

The road to success is not an elevator ride. It is like a

long, exhausting walk up the longest staircase in the world, the Niesen mountain railway staircase. With 11,674 steps, it takes great perseverance to make it to the top.

This is a reality you will need to constantly remind yourself about as you embark on this journey. Perseverance wins the race. Each time you feel like giving up, remember why you started. Keep that vision board prominently placed in your home so that you never lose sight of the road ahead.

Keep those blinkers on.

We understand the odds stacked against us as black American women. It would be great if people judged us based on the quality of our character rather than the color of our skin. Sadly, that is not the world in which we live.

That does not mean, however, that we should succumb to the stereotypes the world places on us. There are several black women who have overcome those stereotypes and achieved unprecedented success. Why shouldn't you be able to do the same?

Ultimately, your ability to glow as an accomplished black woman depends on your ability to persevere. Are you ready to climb those 11,674 steps to make it to the top? There will be a lot of blood, sweat and tears but the reward is what ultimately matters.

Keep those blinkers on and push forward. The prize is yours.

REFLECTION QUESTIONS

1. What is causing you to lose sight of your dreams?
2. What challenges are you presently facing as you work towards your dream?
3. What adjustments do you need to make to overcome your challenges?
4. How can you get rid of the noise in your life so that you can better focus on your goals?

CONCLUSION

I WROTE THIS BOOK because I realized that African American women are underserved in the area of personal development literature. We needed a book written for *us* by someone who understands our daily plight.

Two thoughts crossed my mind as I prepared to write this book.

1. Should I write it as a memoir of my life?
2. Should I write it as a practical guide that any black woman could feel was written specifically for her?

I chose the latter because I realized that the work I am called to do is not all about me. Instead, it is about empowering a community of black women to glow in their marvelous light and make a profound impact in this world. I hope that this book has empowered you to do just that so that you do not allow your unfulfilled dreams to contribute to the wealth of the graveyard.

Several nuggets of wisdom have been shared throughout

this book. However, there are six key takeaways I want you to keep at the forefront of your mind. If you do not remember anything else, remember these six things.

Your ability to glow starts with your mind.

The G.L.O.W Principle has four phases. You cannot jump headfirst into phase four where you walk into your destiny if you have not done the work to deal with your mental battles.

There is nothing wrong with admitting that there are some cobwebs you need to clear from your mind. You have probably allowed them to stay there for too long. It is time to let them go so that you have the mental space to live fully in your purpose.

It is not easy. Cleaning out these cobwebs will force you to confront a lot of hurt and pain you have tried to bury for a long time. Nevertheless, those cobwebs need to go if you want to effectively glow.

Remember, too, that cleaning out those cobwebs is not a one-time event. Sure, you need to take some time to deal with the pain and hurt. Once you do, that will be a burden off your shoulders.

However, there will be times when the cobwebs try to re-enter your mental space. You will also form new cobwebs as life progresses. Therefore, training your mind to think differently and get rid of any cobwebs quickly is important for lasting success.

Support is crucial, you cannot glow alone.

I applaud you for being a strong, black woman who is capable of accomplishing the seemingly impossible. Your strength should be acknowledged and celebrated. However, things become a tad bit easier when you lean on the support of others rather than try to do everything alone.

I have been there, done that and the whole, "I can do this all by myself" mantra really does not fly if you are serious about making your dreams a reality. You need a support network in the form of:

- An accountability partner.
- Mentor(s).
- Active participation in organization that support the causes you care about.

Stereotypes do not define you.

Society bombards us with so many fallacies about who we are and who we should be. We are no longer living in the Jim Crow era where the rights of black Americans were ignored. This is the 21st century and it is time for the world to understand that we are all part of one human race. No ethnicity is superior to another.

The right opportunities are out there for you, so do not allow stereotypes to hold you back. You may have to look a bit harder. But the search will be worth it as you find opportunities that fit with your core values and align with your life's purpose.

If you are in a place where stereotypes are in your face daily, it may be time to leave. Weight the pros and the cons of taking the leap. More importantly, spend a few months preparing for your exit if you do not have any immediate opportunities. Leaps are risky. Preparation helps you better manage the risk so that you can experience success.

Plan. Prepare. Persist.

You may have stopped pursuing your dreams because life got in the way. It is easier to put everyone else's dreams before our own.

Not anymore. It is time for you to do more than planning and preparing. You now need to develop the consistent effort necessary to take small steps towards your vision. Learning to be persistent in your consistency yields results.

Do not downplay the value of the right life partner.

Beautiful relationships are built on a foundation of mutual respect, love and the desire to build each other up. They are not one-sided arrangements where one person is a leech to the other. Instead, the right partners complement each other in ways you probably never even thought was possible, a point that becomes particularly important as you both work towards achieving your dreams.

The thing is, though, that this "right" person will not

come in a perfect package. It is great to have standards, but do not allow those standards to cloud your judgement. Be open to possibilities, look out for red flags and build a connection with someone who is meant to be your partner for life.

Self-care is important.

Demands on your time will increase as you step closer towards your vision. Your family needs you, your friends need you, work needs you, the organizations you join need you and your community of black sisters need you. How do you make time for them while also carving out enough time for yourself?

The best answer to that question is this: make self-care a priority! We discussed how to prioritize your day in Chapter 11. Find the prioritization strategy that works for you so that you can do what you need to do to take care of you.

It is time to step into your marvelous light.

I hope this book is the jolt of energy you needed to start taking your dreams seriously. I hope your eyes have been opened and you have really started putting things in place to G.L.O.W. Life is a journey, it is a long race. Stay in your lane, run at your own pace, and keep moving forward. The best is yet to come.

May I ask you a small favor?

If you enjoyed this book and got helpful pointers and actionable strategies from it, **would you consider letting others know about it?**

Here are several ways you can do so:

>> Leave a quick review on **Amazon US** <<
>> Leave a quick review on **Amazon UK** <<

I would be delighted if you could also:

1. Tell your peeps about it on your **Blog, Podcast,** or **YouTube** Channel
2. Share it on **Facebook, Instagram, Twitter, Pinterest,** or **LinkedIn**
3. Mention it to your **friends and family members,** or your colleagues at work

Reviews on Amazon are incredibly helpful - both for other readers to decide whether this book will be useful to them and for indie authors and publishers to get the word out about our books. Your support is much appreciated!

Thanks in advance for your good deeds!

You are a STAR...:)

Warm regards,

Erika Rae Bailey

Get FREE Books
Before They Are Released!

Join the Insider's Club and we will email you **FREE** copies of new books before we publish them.

You may ask, why would we give away our books for **FREE**?

Well, our ***VIP Insider Club Members*** help us greatly with fine-tuning a book before it goes on general release.

We value any feedback and input provided, whenever it is needed. We have some of the best editors in the business, but now and then, our eagle-eyed Insider Club Members will spot something that could do with a little tweaking…thanks in advance!

We publish non-fiction and fiction books, from business, self-help and health books to children's stories and romance novels.

Click (or tap) below to JOIN the exclusive **VIP Insider Club Members** and start receiving FREE Books before they are published.

Click here:
https://www.mangobroom.com/insiders-club/

REFERENCES

Blackman, A. (2019, February 11). 20 successful companies founded or owned by black entrepreneurs. Envatotuts. https://business.tutsplus.com/articles/successful-companies-black-entrepreneurs--cms-32691

Debaun, M. (2019, July 19). 5 years in: Blavity's next chapter. LinkedIn. https://www.linkedin.com/pulse/5-years-blavitys-next-chapter-morgan-debaun

Meeks, C. (2018, March 26). *How black women describe navigating race and gender in the workplace.* Harvard Business Review. https://hbr.org/2018/03/how-black-women-describe-navigating-race-and-gender-in-the-workplace

Mills, D., Lee, C.W., & Crouse, K. (2016, August 12). G*olden reaction: what Simone Manuel's historic moment looked like*. The New York Times. https://www.nytimes.com/2016/08/13/sports/olympics/simone-manuel-gold-reaction.html

Paul, M., Zaw, K., Hamilton, D., & Darity, W. (2018). *Returns in the labor market: A nuanced view of penalties at the intersection of race and gender*. Washington Center for Equitable Growth. https://equitablegrowth.org/wp-content/uploads/2018/07/080718-WP-intersectionality-labor-market.pdf

Trafton, A. (2014, January 16). *In the blink of an eye: MIT neuroscientists find the brain can identify images seen for as little as 13 milliseconds.* Massachusetts Institute of Technology. https://news.mit.edu/2014/in-the-blink-of-an-eye-0116

Made in the USA
Las Vegas, NV
28 December 2021

39518789R00108